The Joy of Efficiency

The Joy of Efficiency

How to Live and Work Better with Less

Paul Westbrook

Printed in the United States of America

First Printing 2019

ISBN 978-1-7339563-0-7

RE:source
https://resourcedesign.org

Joy (*noun*): a feeling of great pleasure and happiness
https://en.oxforddictionaries.com/definition/joy

Efficiency (*noun*): 1. the state or quality of being efficient, or able to accomplish something with the least waste of time and effort; competency in performance. 2. accomplishment of or ability to accomplish a job with a minimum expenditure of time and effort: 3. the ratio of the work done or energy developed by a machine, engine, etc., to the energy supplied to it, usually expressed as a percentage.
(https://www.dictionary.com/browse/efficiency?s=t)

Dedication

This book is dedicated to all the engineers, designers, craftspeople, and others in the world who see a better way that can benefit everyone, but who have to constantly swim upstream against the status quo.

Acknowledgements

My late mother, Veronica Westbrook, who covered both the mother and father role for my sister and me. She always put us first, ensured we received a good education, took us on great trips that instilled my love of nature, and set a good example of frugality.

My wife, Elena Westbrook. It's no coincidence that almost everything great that occurred in my life happened after we met. She is smart, kind, caring, and thoughtful. We have a unique blend of similarities and differences that help make me a much better person.

My daughter, Kendall Westbrook, who has a great sense of humor and keeps me laughing. Laughter is good for your health and sanity, so she might be unintentionally postponing her inheritance.

The writing of Amory Lovins influenced me long before I met him. His vision, knowledge, enthusiasm, and humor helped me navigate the peril-filled path of instituting major change at a corporation. Whenever I feel like there are too many obstacles, I reread his Applied Hope letter and I'm energized again. (https://rmi.org/wp-content/uploads/2017/05/RMI_Document_Repository_Public-Reprts_Applied-Hope-Letter.pdf)

Shaunna Black gave us permission to dream big at work. She is a rare example of someone practicing servant leadership. Shaunna helped identify and clear the obstacles so we could implement successful solutions that even exceeded our own aggressive goals.

After I designed my house I almost gave up on the idea when I couldn't find a suitable builder. Then I found Richard Harwood. His enthusiasm, experience, and lifelong love of learning got our house built correctly and on budget.

Thanks to my wife for her editing assistance. My friend Lara Wallentine Hussain also helped me edit the book. Finally, Brian Tedesco brought it all together with the final editing and layout and then he guided me through the book publishing process.

Table of Contents

Preface

In 1996, I designed our family's passive solar house, which 22+ years later is still ahead of its time. We have toured more than 1,800 people through the home in two decades, mostly in conjunction with the American Solar Energy Society's National Tour of Solar Homes. Many people who toured the house told me, "You should write a book," but I had a full-time job and there never seemed to be enough time.

When I took an early retirement, I decided I should finally write that book. My professional work had already been highlighted in several books by others: *Hot, Flat, and Crowded* by Thomas Freedman; *Reinventing Fire* by Amory Lovins; and *Influence Without Authority* by Allan Cohen. I thought it was time to tell the whole story about my personal and professional approach to efficient living, myself. Therefore, the book is not only about our house. The house is really more a manifestation of my lifestyle—a lifestyle driven by constantly seeking to find a simpler and more elegant path, a more efficient solution. Everything is connected, so I decided to write about all the quests for efficiency—including the house.

The book contains guidelines and tips, and even some data and formulas. But it also contains stories, because stories are how we best learn and relate to things.

Several people who know much more about books than I do encouraged me to make this into three separate books. But it seemed more efficient to just make one book. And as you'll see, I don't do things just because that's the way they've usually been done.

Once a friend came on our house tour and was commenting on many things we did in the house that were out of the ordinary. Near the end of the tour, we were standing outside the garage when he looked in and saw my recumbent bicycle. He said, "Everything is different at the Westbrook House." And he's correct in many ways. We don't just do something because everyone else is doing it. We seek the best path—even if it's not considered "normal." Seek opportunities to do things more efficiently and embrace them, even if it's not the "normal" path.

—Paul Westbrook, December 23, 2018 (Happy Festivus)

Introduction

People always seem to be short of time or money—sometimes both. Efficiency is a way to get more of both. It's not a compromise; it's an optimization where everything is better. It's a way to live lighter on the planet, and to live better. It's quality versus quantity.

Efficiency rewards you similarly to the way a financial investment grows. Just as compound interest allows your money to grow over time, efficiency's benefits continue to accumulate. Efficiency has a better return with a higher guarantee than any financial investment. Like planting a tree, the best time to start being efficient was twenty years ago; the second-best time is now.

Embracing efficiency is not difficult. It is often just a matter of replacing old, bad habits with new, better habits. To develop a new, good habit you'll have to actively work at it for a month, but then it becomes a new good habit. Develop some new good habits and you, too, will know the *Joy of Efficiency*.

This book has three major sections. If you are interested in organizing your life so you have more time and money, then the first third of the book is for you. It's a bit of a self-help book. If you are interested in building or buying a better house, then the middle third is for you. This section is for those who want to live better for less—and with a much lighter impact on the planet. If you work in a corporation and want to improve your buildings, systems, or your work processes, then the final third is for you. This is the business process and systems section, and it's applicable to many areas of a business or company. Throughout the book, the effective path to efficiency is explained through true stories and examples. We learn best through stories instead of just formulas and data.

This book may seem to ramble across topics, but read enough and you'll find the thread connecting them all. The power of efficiency—and the joy of living an efficient life—lies in those connections.

A reporter once asked me if I considered myself an activist. I thought about it for a few seconds and replied that I consider myself more of a "doivist." An activist works to convince people to change. A doivist implements changes, then shares the success with others, hoping they will follow. I'm sharing my success through this book.

The Power of Efficiency

This book will focus on energy more than any other topic, because energy is fundamental to almost every aspect of our modern society. Fossil fuel energy extraction and trading is also a source of major conflicts around the globe. Consider the U.S. energy consumption for a typical year. Over 60% of the energy produced here is wasted. Our fossil-fuel-driven power plants lose most of their fuel's energy content to waste heat, which is dumped into the atmosphere or local water supplies. Gasoline-powered vehicles waste more than 70% of the fuel's energy content. The majority of the energy we've drilled for, dug up, mined, and otherwise extracted over the past few hundred years has been wasted. We either didn't know how to get more use from our energy source or didn't bother to figure it out. A study by Lawrence Livermore National Laboratory indicates about 67% of the energy input into the U.S. economy is rejected as waste heat, which means we didn't get any useful work from it. This acceptance of inefficiency is a voluntary tax on our collective prosperity—at a tax rate of about 67%. We would revolt if our income tax rate was that high, but we continue to accept that level of waste in our energy system.

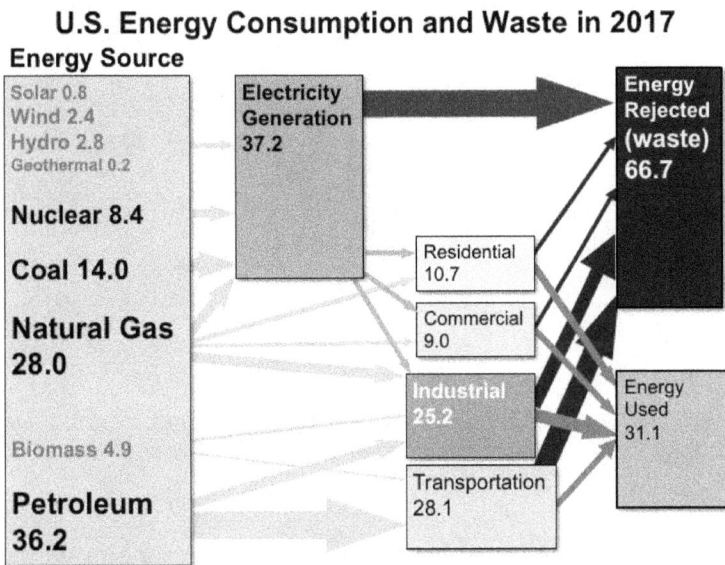

U.S. Energy Consumption and Waste in 2017

Energy Source

Solar 0.8	Electricity Generation 37.2
Wind 2.4	Energy Rejected (waste) 66.7
Hydro 2.8	
Geothermal 0.2	
Nuclear 8.4	Residential 10.7
Coal 14.0	Commercial 9.0
Natural Gas 28.0	Industrial 25.2
	Energy Used 31.1
Biomass 4.9	Transportation 28.1
Petroleum 36.2	

Figure 1. U.S. energy flow and rejected energy. Data from Lawrence Livermore National Labs

https://flowcharts.llnl.gov/content/assets/images/energy/us/Energy_US_2017.png

As Amory Lovins at the Rocky Mountain Institute (RMI) has pointed out for decades, saving energy is cheaper than buying energy; energy efficiency costs less than the fuel it saves. And there are many cascading benefits: our finances, our air quality, our water quality and availability, our health…

We have made some progress, but efficiency is still probably the greatest business opportunity of our time. But it is more than a business opportunity. It is a chance to do well by doing good. When we, as a society, become more efficient, everyone wins. A more efficient food supply chain could feed more people with what we already grow. More efficient transportation systems could move more people with even less energy.

Efficiency wins might manifest as cost savings, clean air, clean water—or even just access to water. Efficiency won't solve all our challenges, but it's the fundamental baseline that all other solutions could build from. If there were a Maslow's hierarchy of energy, efficiency would be the broad base of the pyramid.

Efficiency is so powerful and applicable to so many things I'm surprised Stan Lee never created a character whose superpower was efficiency.

Figure 2. Efficiency superhero. Unisex stick figure for efficient use of ink. The Greek letter Eta (η) is often used to denote efficiency.

Of course, people might have called it Eta Man (or Eta Woman, or Eta Person), which doesn't exactly have a superhero ring to it.

Measurement

How do you know how efficient or inefficient you are? You have to use data and a bit of scientific method.

Data is the currency of efficiency. But don't panic—it's doesn't have to be overly complicated data. We live in an age where there is an abundance, if not an excess, of data available. You can use something as simple as paper and pencil for many things. A simple spreadsheet is often very effective. For example, in 1983, I began logging data for my car every time I filled up with gas. I had a little pad and pen in the car to record the info—miles driven, gallons purchased, and cost per gallon. With that data, I would calculate my miles per gallon for each tank. Over time, this helped me understand the effect driving habits had on fuel efficiency. It also helped me note the car needed maintenance when I saw a consistent drop in mileage. When personal computers and spreadsheet programs arrived, I began to log this data into a spreadsheet, which allowed me to add charts and get a better visual feel for the data. As the internet blossomed and local weather data became available, I started logging the average temperature across each tank. Now, there are free apps you can put on your phone and just enter the info right after you fill up. The charts are all produced automatically for you online or in your app.

The same process applies to monitoring your household energy and utility use. You can log your bills on a piece of paper or enter them in a spreadsheet. Many utilities have online sites now that allow you to view your energy and/or water consumption. As I once told someone, without data you're just making stuff up.

Once you have basic data on consumption and cost, you can keep it simple or get a little more sophisticated and include variables such as weather, recent maintenance, tire pressure, etc. I'll leave the complexity level up to you, but you really should keep at least a basic analysis. It's similar to your finances—if you don't know where your money is going, you can't make a good plan for how to save money and manage your finances. If you don't know where your energy use is going, you're not going to be very successful at reducing your consumption.

Some of the data I monitor are:

1. **Spending.** I use an online financial aggregation website and have all my financial data fed there. After a couple of years of data collection, I had an excellent picture of where my money was going. Being honest about your actual spending is the first step to making some positive changes.

2. **Household energy and water use and cost.** I track and trend these via a spreadsheet and a real-time energy monitoring system. I also track my solar electric production via a separate real-time monitoring system. All the data are downloaded to a spreadsheet for more detailed analysis. I also import the weather data from a National Weather Service site so I can normalize the data to account for weather fluctuations.

3. **Car mileage.** I log every tank. There are many phone apps you can use to simplify this. I use an app for quick entry, then later dump the data to a spreadsheet for further analysis.

4. **Major costs.** On my utility tracking spreadsheet, I also have a tab where I track a few major cost items. I log my house valuation and property tax each year, along with my annual homeowner's and auto insurance rates. It's interesting to watch some of these costs creep up slowly over time—or sometimes quite rapidly. For insurance, I'll call and get competitive quotes and ratchet them back down again. In the case of property taxes, it becomes obvious if one entity is rising much faster than others, and I can use the data to ask that taxing entity why they can't manage their costs better. If I weren't tracking these, the subtle annual changes might go unnoticed.

You'll find examples of several of these tracking mechanisms throughout the book. If you need to start with a Big Chief tablet and a pencil, that's OK. Just start logging the data and add as much history as you can find. People are not very good at accurately estimating or even remembering what they are spending money on. Log it and let the data speak the truth and be your guide.

Everyday Life

Time

I'm covering time at the beginning because it is the most valuable to me. Time only moves in one direction—forward. And it waits for no one. Who doesn't want more time to do the fun things in life, to spend with loved ones, or to simply do nothing? We certainly all need money to live, but there is a certain level of income and savings that can provide a good life with minimal stress.

Chasing more money after a certain point is probably not the best path. Besides, if you live efficiently, you'll live well on less money. Look for balance instead. Seek more time for yourself, your family, and your friends. Time could be considered currency the same way money is. Strive to be time-wealthy.

There are many ways to optimize your time. First, you need recognize time's value. When I was searching for land to build our house, I found two parcels that I liked, and they had a significant price difference. One parcel was about eight miles farther out from my office than the other, but it had a much lower price. Once I assigned a monetary value to my time, the closer parcel was a much better value despite the higher initial price. Looking back, I think I even undervalued my time. Over twenty years I would have spent at least an extra half-hour per day commuting round-trip. Over two decades, that is an extra 2,300 hours sitting in a car. That's over three months of time. And then there is the extra gasoline and wear and tear that additional 73,000 miles of commuting would have added over twenty years, not to mention the stress of traffic. Worse, that added mileage calculation only included my commute to work. Add in additional mileage to purchase groceries and basics, to attend events or visit friends, and it adds up to even more lost time. Then add in my wife's commute, and we would have lost almost a year of life commuting in twenty years of living. Assign a cost value to your time as another way to view it. Even a modest hourly value of $20/hour times 2,300 hours equals $46,000.

The ideal situation would have been to find a parcel of land or a well-designed house very near my office so I could have walked or bicycled to work. But there were not any adequate or affordable parcels close to the office, and finding a well-designed home was next to impossible, as you'll see later in the book.

There are many ways to optimize your time, and planning ahead is a big part. That brings me to one of my sayings: "Plan ahead, get ahead." I used to say this around my daughter all the time. Initially she mocked it, but as she got older she began to realize the value, and now she is a big proponent of the philosophy. She embraced it because she observed the value planning brings to so many areas of life—from commuting to vacations to home design and more.

One of the simplest time optimizations is to combine errands and trips. If you run errands on the way home from work instead of making an extra trip out on the weekend, you'll free up some additional time. It's an easy change to make, and it just requires a little advance planning. While I was working and commuting, I rarely used my car on the weekends—I ran errands on the way home from work while I was already out and often driving right past the store. I usually just exercise from my house—jog, run, bicycle, shoot baskets in the driveway. It beats adding time to drive to a fitness facility. If you are driving somewhere every day, set a goal of not using your car at all one day per week.

We didn't have rigid start/stop times for most of my work years, so I really optimized my time by shifting my commuting hours. My commute distance was just over 18 miles each way, mostly on a highway—a very busy highway. With minimal traffic, I could be door to door in 25 minutes—or even a little less. During rush hour (which actually lasts about three to four hours in the morning and again in the afternoon), it could take closer to an hour each way. I was usually at work before 7:00 in the morning, so I rode the front of the traffic bubble to keep the commute closer to thirty minutes. I also usually packed a lunch and ate at my desk. Early arrival and short lunches allowed me to get out well before 4:00 P.M. on most days and keep the drive home about thirty minutes, too. And on Tuesday and Thursday I would go in even earlier and play basketball at our on-site fitness center. We started about 6:00 in the morning, which still allowed me to get to work early after a good workout. Shortening the commute times and fitting in my exercise was very time-efficient. And having a fitness center at our work site had tremendous value for the employees who chose to use it.

There are many organizational systems, from a calendar on the refrigerator to an electronic schedule synchronized to every device you own, including a high-tech refrigerator. It really doesn't matter which one you use; just find one that works for you and your household and stick with it until organizing your time becomes a good habit. If you follow some of the other efficiency areas in the book, you'll see some time free up in other ways as well. I drive a very efficient car, which means I stop for gasoline less than half as often as most motorists. Yes, it might just be ten minutes here and there I save, but over years and decades, that time adds up. And it also lowers the chance of additional impulse spending at the gas station. It's all connected.

There are also apps that can help you manage your online time. You might not need anything fancy. If you find yourself on social media way too often, then set an egg timer and start checking your accounts. When the timer goes off, shut the screen down and walk away. Developing self-discipline in any area of your life can help you build it in other areas.

Great joy can be found from managing your time well. The greatest joy comes from things that happen in that free time you create. Creating time for a couple of walks each day with my dog is more of a benefit for me than it is for the dog. A simple walk is good for your physical health and your mental health.

Great joy can be found from managing your time well.
The greatest joy comes from things that happen
in that free time you create.

Imagine what would happen if organizations, companies, and government recognized the value of time and made things as simple as possible. That would free up large amounts of time for everyone to pursue important and joyful things. I could write an entire chapter on efficiency in meetings. Imagine the freedom of reducing bureaucratic burdens, from streamlining building permits to radical tax simplification, and all the free time those changes could provide every tax-paying citizen—not to mention the reduced stress.

Money

What is money? Money is just a medium of exchange, or as poet William Matthews said, "Money is math with consequences" (from *Time and Money,* Houghton Mifflin, 1995). Before the invention of money, people bartered for things: "I'll give this to you if you'll give me that" (or do this task). Money is now the way we trade for things. But acquiring money has also grown into an obsession for many people. And our money has evolved from cash, to paper (usually in the form of a check), to electrons traded online.

Sometimes, usually around election time, I think I would like to just build an off-the-grid house out away from everyone and drop out of society. Just stop playing the game. Check out of the system. It's very tempting. But, since I've chosen to stay in the game, then I want to win—or at least finish well. For better or worse, money is how our society tends to measure things. Money is both our primary currency and unfortunate scorecard. When I see the annual *Parade* magazine "What they Earn" issue, I always want to change it to "What they are Paid." I'm not sure that a person who hits a small ball with a stick is really *earning* 200 times more money than a good teacher, but that's what our society has accepted, and that's what they are paid. Are people who throw, catch, and hit a ball really worth that much to society? What people are paid is not always in line with their actual value to humanity. The real question to ask is, "What are we valuing?" But I digress and am starting to think about dropping out of society again.

It's hard to control what you get paid, but you do have quite a bit of control over what you spend. And that is the key—how efficiently you spend your money, regardless of your income. Aspire to be frugal. Frugality should not be confused with being cheap. Frugal people focus on getting the most value from their money. Learning to manage your spending will allow you to live much better and more joyfully. The top three areas of spending for most people are housing, transportation, and food. Hopefully, shopping for stuff like clothes, furniture and electronics doesn't eclipse any of these. If shopping for stuff is one of your top spending categories, I would suggest you check out *The Story of Stuff* by Annie Leonard (https://storyofstuff.org/).

Speaking of "stuff," most of us have too much stuff. Way too much stuff. When your car won't fit in the garage or you have to rent a space somewhere to put your extra stuff, then you probably need to take a hard look at your choices. Stuff, and storing it, is an inefficient use of your time. Buying too much stuff and paying to store it is an inefficient use of both your money and your time. There are many books and methods that talk about simplifying and decluttering your life. Ideally, you wouldn't build up clutter in the first place, but either way, there is joy to be gained by reducing your stuff. I would rather own a few high-quality items than an array of essentially disposable things. And if you don't distribute all your money to buy many useless things, you'll be able to afford higher quality for the items you do purchase.

Many of the things people purchase comes from the "keeping up with the Joneses" factor. Since I'm not concerned about what type of car my neighbor drives, how big their house is, or how expensive their TV is, I am free to make good decisions without that negative influence.

Financial planners will tell you that you should put a small amount of money into savings every month. Over time this money will grow and compound. If you save money by being energy-efficient or buying less stuff, the savings will compound in a similar fashion.

It does take some work and discipline to get on the right financial path. You have to develop a plan, make a few tough choices, and stick with your plan. The joy comes after several years of hard work, when your accounts have grown and you feel like you have a little cushion in life. Eventually, these savings can grow enough to make your job optional. It's a pretty joyous feeling to go to work because you want to and not because you have to. If things aren't going your way, you can just move on. And that's exactly what I did.

Live-Beneath-Your-Means Savings Plan

I realize some people are barely getting by, but the vast majority of us can live well on less. When I started work right out of college, I set up an automatic savings deposit with about 30% of my paycheck. Every time I got a raise, I increased the amount I put in savings. Sometimes the entire raise went to savings, and sometimes I rewarded myself with a little additional spending money. Once you learn to live on less, you won't even notice all the money automatically depositing in savings. That savings should ideally be broken into three categories: near term, medium term, and long term (retirement). Many financial advisors will wisely recommend you build up an emergency fund of about three to six months of living expenses first—your near-term savings. After that, begin contributing to your three savings buckets, and over time, as they grow, they will become your emergency savings for large or small issues that might arise.

Near-term savings could also be used for a fun vacation, a modest purchase, or an unexpected issue. Such savings are usually invested in an insured savings account for easy access. The account may not be earning much money, but it's not going to lose any, either. This cash is accumulating and quickly accessible.

The medium-term savings is for big purchases such as a house, car, or kid's college education. This money can be invested in the stock market, bonds, etc. With this savings category, your timeline is longer to ride out market fluctuations.

Long-term savings is generally retirement savings. There are many books, articles, and experts talking about savings plans, so I won't spend a lot of time on the topic. I'll say the most important thing I've learned is: Do it. Start saving right away and use raises as an opportunity to increase savings. You can manage it yourself. Look for low-cost investments, such as low-cost mutual funds or index funds that allow you to have a diverse portfolio. Have a little diversity in your savings and rebalance the funds every year or two. Set up regular and automatic deposits into those funds. Don't think you can time the market and beat it. Over time, slow and steady investing almost always wins—and it's much less stressful to manage than actively playing market swings.

Good money management also allows you not to care about your credit score. If I'm not planning to borrow money, I have no use for a formulaic opinion of some financial institutions. I once tried to work through the system to fix an overzealous medical bill. After months of zero progress, I finally decided I wouldn't pay it. It wasn't that much money, and I could have paid it, but it was the principle. When they gave me the "this will hurt your credit score" threat, I just laughed. My credit score is still excellent despite that one nonpayment, but I really don't care. Ironically, part of your credit score is based on how many credit cards you have—my report actually dings me a bit for having too few cards. Seems like a self-promoting industry tactic. Unfortunately, the system can be stacked against you, as your score is sometimes used by insurance companies to set your rates (in states where that tactic is legal). If you are applying for a mortgage, the credit score is used not only to determine if you'll get a loan, but what interest rate you will pay. A modified version of the credit report can be requested by potential employers, as well. If you can get to the point that you can be your own bank, then you have more freedom to avoid this industry game.

For good, practical financial advice, I've enjoyed Scott Burns' columns over the years: https://assetbuilder.com/knowledge-center/articles/authors/scott-burns.

Burns' investing advice site is Couch Potato Investing: https://couchpotatoinvesting.com/. He's very pragmatic and does a good job of helping you efficiently save your money. Dave Ramsey also provides good, practical financial advice (https://www.daveramsey.com/).

"Look How Much I Saved!"—When a Bargain Is No Bargain

If you are thinking about how much you are saving with a coupon or sale price, then you are doing it wrong. What do you have to spend to get that "savings?" Buying something because it's on sale or is a perceived "good deal" is wrong. Only clip coupons for things you were actually planning to purchase—don't buy something because you have a coupon. Don't go to a sale because you see such a great deal. Decide what you really need first, then search for the best price/value.

If you are thinking about how much you are saving with a coupon or sale price, then you are doing it wrong.

I have a pretty methodical approach to any purchase. When I've decided I need something, or, occasionally, want something, I follow the same general plan:

- Research first to find reviews and reliability data. Unbiased sources like *Consumer Reports* are a good place to gather information. I always use multiple sources. If it's an appliance, I also use the Energy Star ratings to narrow the list. A little research helps me narrow choices down to a top list for consideration. I look for reliable, functional choices that represent the best value.
- Make another research pass looking for consumer reviews on the narrowed list of manufacturers or models of the item. Sometimes I'll even make a quick comparison spreadsheet.

- Once you have a list of high-quality finalists with the features you need, start considering price.
- Search for the best price among the top choices.

Note the goal is not to buy the cheapest item. This process often eliminates the cheap items that won't last very long, because something you have to replace frequently is not really a low-cost choice. I'm searching for the best value. Deal searching will include web searches, price comparison sites, and coupon sites. Remember, I'm searching for a coupon AFTER I've chosen the product. I often find a little bit of research can get a higher quality product at close to the price of a cheaply made version.

When you buy a quality product, you have absolutely no need for the "extended warranty" plan. If you follow my savings advice, you'll always have money saved for an emergency repair. You become self-warrantied. The retailers make a profit from those warranties; otherwise, they wouldn't offer them. For every person who says they had a claim honored on an extended warranty, there were many more who paid and got nothing. Be your own warranty provider and pay yourself.

Counting Pennies

If you poke a thousand small holes in a water tower, the water will drain out just as fast as if you made one large hole. It's the same with spending. It's the small items that add up to make you wonder where your money went. For example, I packed my lunch almost every day for my entire 33-year working career. Assume I did this for 220 days a year. The ingredients for a sandwich, chips, fruit, trail mix, and yogurt add to less than $2. And I always drank water—no sodas. If I had eaten in the cafeteria or at a restaurant I would easily have spent at least $6 per day more. Six dollars multiplied by 220 days per year for 33 years comes to more than $43,000 in savings, not counting any interest I might have earned from investing those dollars instead of spending them. In addition, my health benefited (and healthcare costs were presumably reduced) because my lunches were nutritious without loading up on too many calories.

There are many daily, weekly, or monthly small expenditures that can add up to a lot of money over the course of a year. When we moved to our house in 1996, we decided to drop cable TV initially and see if we missed it. We found we could live fine without it. There were dozens of local broadcast

TV stations available for free over the airwaves. When I wanted an over-the-air TV recording device, I found one that didn't require a monthly subscription fee. I'm very hesitant about any products that charge ongoing fees. Those fees can often add to more than the initial product cost in just a couple of years. Make a spreadsheet or use one of the many online financial aggregation programs to collect all your spending data and analyze it. It may hold some surprises about where your money is really going.

Live for Free

When I retired after 33+ years, I added up all my income from salary, bonuses, stock options, etc., then added my wife's income since we've been married. I assumed a 20% net tax rate (although with income, property, social security, Medicare, and sales tax, the total is actually much, much higher). When I compared that total income to our net worth, it turned out we still have all our earnings—and quite a bit more. Some of it is invested in our house, but we own that free and clear. It has cost us nothing to live over the past third of a century, and we've lived quite well. If you spend below your income, save and invest well, you can grow as much money as you spend and live well for free. Certainly, we spend more than $0 per year to live, but our savings and investment income eventually offset all that spending. It's not a get-rich-quick scheme—it's a live-rich-slow plan.

You might be able to do this, too, if you follow the advice in this book. Set up a good savings plan, make a few mainstream investments, and spend your money wisely in all aspects of your life. You'll see the efficiency savings compound over the years and decades. Even if you don't manage to live for free, you'll still be way ahead and have a solid financial cushion.

It's not a get-rich-quick scheme, it's a live-rich-slow plan.

A big piece of my strategy is not to borrow money. I have credit cards, but I use them for convenience (and expense tracking) and pay them off fully every month. I've never paid any interest to a credit card company. In fact, with the 2% cashback card I use, the credit card company pays me. The only time I ever borrowed money was to purchase a house, and I paid that back quickly by making extra principle payments.

Home Finance

Housing is probably where most of us spend the largest amount of money, so it is a great place to start improving your financial situation. The big question for most people is whether to buy or rent. And the answers are so varied I won't pretend to have a formula for everyone. Whichever route you choose, the key is not to stretch yourself too far. (Modesty is a virtue, in homes as in everything else.) And if you buy, then try to minimize your borrowing—in both the amount and the duration. Since the economic crash of 2008, we've had extraordinarily low interest rates, but when you take out a loan, you are still paying someone else to use their money, which puts an obligation hanging over your head. Make your loan for as short a duration as you can (rates are usually lower on a 15-year mortgage versus a 30-year loan), then make extra principal payments to shorten the actual duration. This approach will reduce the amount of interest you pay.

Table 1 (following page) illustrates how mortgage payments work. The example compares a 15-year loan at 4% and a 30-year loan at 4.5%. (Shorter-term home loan rates are generally a little lower.) In the side by side examples, you can see how much faster the shorter-term loan pays down the principal. The table displays each month of the first year, the end of the 15th year (when the 15-year loan is paid off), and the final year of the 30-year loan. And for eagle-eyed readers who note that sometimes the principal and interest don't exactly add to the payment, I rounded to avoid penny overload in the columns. It all adds up accurately.

Note the monthly payment amount is higher for the 15-year loan, but the amount owed drops much faster. In the 15th year, when the shorter duration loan is paid off, the person with the 30-year loan still owes $132,458. During the early years of a 30-year loan, the vast majority of the payment goes toward interest. This keeps the principal balance high for a longer period. At the end, the homeowner with a 30-year loan has paid almost $100,000 more in interest.

That $200,000 loan costs you a total of $266,288 with a 15-year loan and $364,813 with a 30-year loan. Even though the additional $466/month might be tough for some people to afford, you can use good design to save quite a bit each month on utility payments, which frees up money to apply to the mortgage. If the 30-year interest rate were the same as the 15-year rate, then you could take out the 30-year loan to gain some flexibility, then make extra principal payments each month to shorten the payoff. However, you must have the discipline to set up those extra principal payments.

Table 1. Home loan duration and interest rate comparison

Mortgage Payoff Comparison: 15-year versus 30-year loan

| Month | 15 year 4.0% | | | | 30 year 4.5% | | | |
	Payment	Interest	Principal	Balance	Payment	Interest	Principal	Balance
0				$ 200,000				$ 200,000
1	$ 1,479	$ 667	$ 813	$ 199,187	$ 1,013	$ 750	$ 263	$ 199,737
2	$ 1,479	$ 664	$ 815	$ 198,372	$ 1,013	$ 749	$ 264	$ 199,472
3	$ 1,479	$ 661	$ 818	$ 197,554	$ 1,013	$ 748	$ 265	$ 199,207
4	$ 1,479	$ 659	$ 821	$ 196,733	$ 1,013	$ 747	$ 266	$ 198,941
5	$ 1,479	$ 656	$ 824	$ 195,909	$ 1,013	$ 746	$ 267	$ 198,673
6	$ 1,479	$ 653	$ 826	$ 195,083	$ 1,013	$ 745	$ 268	$ 198,405
7	$ 1,479	$ 650	$ 829	$ 194,254	$ 1,013	$ 744	$ 269	$ 198,136
8	$ 1,479	$ 648	$ 832	$ 193,422	$ 1,013	$ 743	$ 270	$ 197,865
9	$ 1,479	$ 645	$ 835	$ 192,587	$ 1,013	$ 742	$ 271	$ 197,594
10	$ 1,479	$ 642	$ 837	$ 191,750	$ 1,013	$ 741	$ 272	$ 197,321
11	$ 1,479	$ 639	$ 840	$ 190,910	$ 1,013	$ 740	$ 273	$ 197,048
12	$ 1,479	$ 636	$ 843	$ 190,067	$ 1,013	$ 739	$ 274	$ 196,774
180	$ 1,479	$ 5	$ 1,474	$ (0)	$ 1,013	$ 499	$ 515	$ 132,468
349					$ 1,013	$ 45	$ 969	$ 10,900
350					$ 1,013	$ 41	$ 972	$ 9,928
351					$ 1,013	$ 37	$ 976	$ 8,952
352					$ 1,013	$ 34	$ 980	$ 7,972
353					$ 1,013	$ 30	$ 983	$ 6,988
354					$ 1,013	$ 26	$ 987	$ 6,001
355					$ 1,013	$ 23	$ 991	$ 5,010
356					$ 1,013	$ 19	$ 995	$ 4,016
357					$ 1,013	$ 15	$ 998	$ 3,017
358					$ 1,013	$ 11	$ 1,002	$ 2,015
359					$ 1,013	$ 8	$ 1,006	$ 1,010
360					$ 1,013	$ 4	$ 1,010	$ (0)
Total	$ 266,288	$ 66,288	$ 200,000		$ 364,813	$ 164,813	$ 200,000	

You can recreate the table above in a spreadsheet program. The formulas are shown in Table 2, below. The first column is just the months. The second column has the payment formula (PMT). Making the balance negative returns a positive number for the payment. The interest is the rate per month (rate divided by 12). The 180 is the number of payment periods (15 years x 12 months/year). The 200,000 is the loan amount. The third column is the interest payment, which is calculated by multiplying the loan amount owed (balance) by the interest rate divided by 12. For the first month, it is 200,000 x 0.04/12. The *Principal* is the *Payment* minus the *Interest*. The *Balance* is the amount owed the previous month minus the *Principal*.

Table 2. Home loan table calculation formulas

Mortgage Payback Comparison Formulas

15 year	0.04				30 year	0.045		
Month	Payment	Interest	Principal	Balance	Payment	Interest	Principal	Balance
0				200000				200000
1	=PMT(D$2/12,180,-F$4)	=F4*D$2/12	=C5-D5	=F4-E5	=PMT(H$2/12,360,-J$4)	=J4*H$2/12	=G5-H5	=J4-I5
2	=PMT(D$2/12,180,-F$4)	=F5*D$2/12	=C6-D6	=F5-E6	=PMT(H$2/12,360,-J$4)	=J5*H$2/12	=G6-H6	=J5-I6
3	=PMT(D$2/12,180,-F$4)	=F6*D$2/12	=C7-D7	=F6-E7	=PMT(H$2/12,360,-J$4)	=J6*H$2/12	=G7-H7	=J6-I7
4	=PMT(D$2/12,180,-F$4)	=F7*D$2/12	=C8-D8	=F7-E8	=PMT(H$2/12,360,-J$4)	=J7*H$2/12	=G8-H8	=J7-I8

copy formulas down

Table 2. Home loan table calculation formulas

If you know where you really want to live, you can stretch a little to get there, especially if you plan to stay. Stretching to live stably in one location is usually better than frequent moves. It costs money and time to change residences. You'll always hear stories about people who benefit from flipping houses, but true long-term success stories are rare. The sooner we stop thinking of our homes as investments, the better off we'll be. Your home is where you live—it's your shelter, which is the fundamental base of Maslow's hierarchy of needs. Don't gamble with your fundamental base. Frequent moving hasn't done much to help build communities, either. People who are transient usually aren't as invested in the long-term health of the neighborhood or community.

When you become a homeowner you also have to be prepared to absorb a wide array of additional costs: taxes, insurance, utilities, maintenance, and more. Utilities can be managed with efficiency (more on that in the house design section). Think about how efficiency plays into the home-buying process. If you purchase a very efficient home, you'll spend less on utility bills. You can choose to apply some of that savings to the mortgage—either to spend a little more on a house or pay down the loan faster. Maintenance can be managed by making the best decision on an array of choices. We choose high-quality, long-life materials. Our philosophy is always to do it well once, and then don't worry about it for a long time.

Insurance is another cost of owning a home. Insurance is basically a legalized form of gambling. When you purchase insurance, you are betting something is going to go wrong or happen to you. We've always used high deductibles to lower our premium and self-insure for the minor issues. If you manage to get some substantial savings built up, you can cut down on all the money you are paying to other organizations and self-insure for many items. Enrich yourself, not your insurance company.

Property taxes can be managed somewhat by not falling into the trap that more square footage is good. Bigger houses cost more to build and operate, and they are usually appraised for more on the tax rolls by a system that values quantity over quality. If you build the right-sized house, it will cost you less and you'll save on property taxes every year.

Life Insurance

If you are fairly young and have someone depending on your income, you might consider purchasing life insurance. However, if you follow my plan of efficiency you'll quickly start accumulating savings—savings that could be used by your family in case something happened to you. At some point you should stop enriching insurance companies and just be self-insured. You can keep adding to your own savings with the premium you aren't paying to a corporation.

Transportation Efficiency and Finance

If you can avoid owning a vehicle, with all the associated costs, then you'll be way ahead of most people. Walking, bicycling, public transportation, or shared rides can be far less expensive if you can make them work for your particular situation.

The Dallas area was built around the vehicle, making it somewhat difficult to function without a car. However, Dallas resident Katie Myers made an intentional choice to live here without owning a car. She first made the car-free choice when she was in college and realized that parking constraints made it easier for her to walk/bike to class than drive and park. After graduation, Katie moved to Chicago, which had enough mass transit to make living without a car workable. Katie explained it best, "It was a smart financial and physical decision for me. It promoted my physical activity and also gave me great levels of mental clarity—not being stuck in miserable traffic."

When Katie moved to a job in the Dallas area, she made it work by moving close to her office. When she changed jobs she even broke her lease so she could move closer to her new office location. There was a financial penalty to do that, but over the year she still comes out well ahead. I've reviewed a number of studies on the actual cost of owning a car, and in Texas and they ranged from \$8,800/year to \$11,700 per year. Katie estimates her annual transportation cost at about \$3,700, but \$960 of that is a transit pass which her employer covers. She uses a variety of forms of transportation: the transit pass, which covers local light rail and bus; free streetcars; Uber/Lyft; an occasional car rental; a shared car service (Zipcar); and even rental scooters.

Katie has, however, had to make a few adjustments. She purchases small amounts of groceries every few days instead of a large weekly trip. She has to allot a little more time and planning to her travel and utilize her transit apps to optimize her connections. Bad weather days make it less enjoyable. But overall, she said, "I really love living without a car. I mean, it is obviously a challenge in Dallas, but I have made it work for a while and I wouldn't change it for anything. I do pay a bit more in rent to live so close to work, but I think I am coming out very much ahead by not having to pay a car note, gas, tolls, maintenance, registration, insurance, parking, etc."

Some people are fortunate to live in, or intentionally move to, a walkable or bikeable area. Others have been clever about figuring out how to get around without a car—either by desire (like Katie) or necessity. Unfortunately, most of the U.S. has developed to be car-centric. A car would be considered a terrible investment if it were a financial product, because it loses value quickly. However, we've developed most areas so that it's almost a necessity.

I've always purchased cars with cash. I know you can sometimes get a good car loan rate, but I prefer to be my own bank. I had a working car when I started my first job, so I saved money like crazy in the first few years. When it came time for a new vehicle, I had enough money to purchase the car I wanted. Then, instead of making car payments, I just kept paying my savings account to build up enough money for the next car. I made car payments to myself. Once you get ahead, you can stay ahead. "Plan ahead, get ahead."

There are a few other items you should consider. One is to buy a reliable car that will last for a long time. I always review the reliability data from sources such as *Consumer Reports*. Vehicles depreciate quickly, so all those extra years you can get out of a reliable, low-maintenance car allow you to keep saving longer. Second, buy a very efficient car to keep the operating costs low. The third tip is to buy a slightly used but reliable car. Someone else absorbs the early depreciation and you get a great deal. You'll still enjoy a long service life by choosing a reliable vehicle. Plus, that new-car smell will have dissipated with a slightly used vehicle. People like a new car smell because they associate that with having a new car. However, that odor is off-gassing of plastics and other materials in your car, and it's not good for your health.

Our family has a fleet of three Toyota Prius vehicles. The first, a 2004 model, was handed down to our daughter and sold in 2018 when she purchased a Prius Prime. Next, we purchased a 2006 model, which my wife sold in 2018 when she also purchased a Prius Prime. Finally, a 2007, which I bought slightly used after handing down the 2004 to our daughter. I'm still driving the 2007 in late-2018.

I've been driving a Prius since August 2004, and as of August 2018, I've saved more than $8,200 in gasoline expenses versus a 25-mpg vehicle. My 14-year average is 54.1 mpg. How do I know this? I keep detailed data on every fill up. I get a little better mileage than the average Prius driver because I operate it efficiently. A few simple driving adjustments can greatly boost the mileage of any car. Learning to look ahead for traffic signals or slowing traffic and coasting is one technique. Driving the speed limit instead of well above reduces aerodynamic drag and improves highway mileage. Keeping tires properly inflated and using low rolling resistance tires will also boost mileage.

Finally, our fleet of Prius cars has been extremely reliable. The car decelerates by using the motor generator to recapture energy, which means the brake pads last for many years. All three of our older cars were still operating on the original brake pads—one of them at 200,000 miles. The reliability means we don't spend much money or time on car repairs—or, even worse, sitting on the side of the road in a broken-down car.

I'm a big fan of data, and I collect and track a lot of information that helps me optimize my life. I've logged every tank of gas I've purchased since 1983. With the Prius, it's allowed me to analyze several factors and further boost my efficiency. My Prius data is updated at https://enerjazz.com/prius.

Here are a few key data points as of mid-2018:

- Lifetime efficiency (>14.0 years and 145,000 miles) = 54.1 mpg
- Gas saved (vs. a 25-mpg car) = >3,200 gallons
- Gas cost savings = $8,200
- Total maintenance cost, including routine maintenance = $3,570

Analyzing the 2007 Prius, which was purchased used, here is the breakdown of cost per mile after my nine years and 78,000 miles of ownership. The purchase cost per mile will continue to decline as I drive additional miles:

Purchase $/mile:	$0.215
Gas $/mile:	$0.029
Insurance $/mile:	$0.060
Maintenance $/mile:	$0.026
Inspection $/mile:	$0.004
Total $/mile:	**$0.334**

For comparison, the IRS mileage reimbursement rate is 54.5 cents per mile in 2018.

When I purchased the lightly used 2007 Prius, the dealership had just put new tires on the car. They chose some cheap tires and did not get the low rolling resistance (LRR) tires that efficient vehicles use. This gave me a great chance to collect some data for a few years before the cheap tires wore out, then compare them to a quality set of LRR replacement tires. The LRR tires provided between 2 and 3.5 mpg better performance, depending on temperature. A 5% improvement in mpg is pretty significant payback for simply paying attention to the tire specifications.

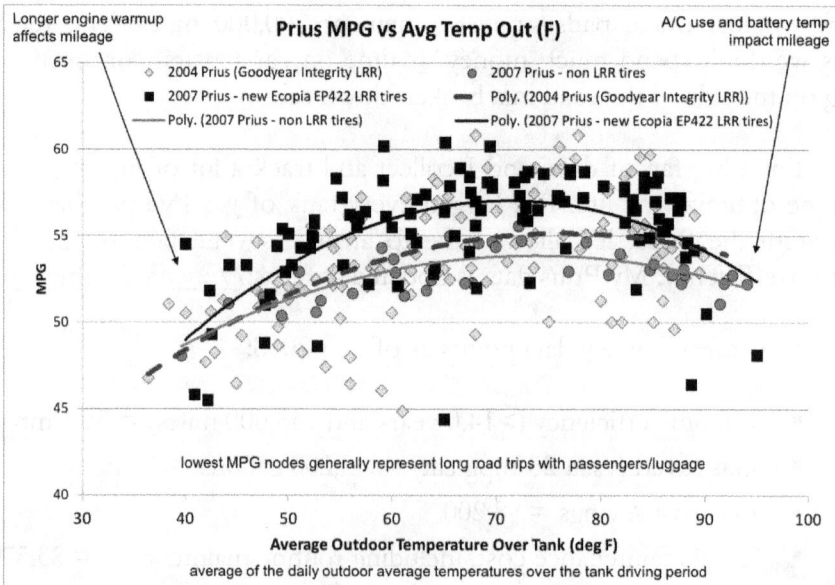

Prius MPG vs Avg Temp Out (F)

Longer engine warmup affects mileage

A/C use and battery temp impact mileage

- ◇ 2004 Prius (Goodyear Integrity LRR)
- ● 2007 Prius - non LRR tires
- ■ 2007 Prius - new Ecopia EP422 LRR tires
- — Poly. (2004 Prius (Goodyear Integrity LRR))
- — Poly. (2007 Prius - non LRR tires)
- — Poly. (2007 Prius - new Ecopia EP422 LRR tires)

MPG

lowest MPG nodes generally represent long road trips with passengers/luggage

Average Outdoor Temperature Over Tank (deg F)

average of the daily outdoor average temperatures over the tank driving period

Figure 3. Prius mileage versus outdoor temperature

Figure 3 plots the tank mpg (calculated from fill-ups, not the display on the dashboard) versus the outdoor temperature for three different vehicle/tire combinations. The blue line is the 2004 Prius with Goodyear Integrity tires. The red line is the 2007 Prius with regular low-cost tires (Primewell PS830) supplied by the dealer. The orange line is the 2007 Prius with LRR tires. I've used Bridgestone Ecopia EP422 tires on this vehicle. The top and bottom end of the temperature ranges were long trips at highway speed in the heat or cold. The middle data points are usually mixed driving and are more representative of actual performance. There are many more charts updated on my website.

It gives me great joy to fill up less than once per month with less than ten gallons of gas. While others complain and fret about gas prices, it is one of my very minor expenses. Driving an efficient vehicle is good for my finances as well as the shared air we breathe and water we drink. Since I retired, I'm using about ten gallons of gas every seven weeks. Electric cars seem to finally be reaching a sales volume that will drive further improvements. I imagine that my next car will be electric, charged from solar panels at my house. At that point, I will produce almost all of my house and vehicle energy with no fossil fuels, and at a substantial cost savings. I'm still puzzled how people claim we can't get away from fossil fuels when it has already become economically disadvantageous to cling to them. We're not making that change overnight, but over the course of many years. Each decision we make puts us in a better position to complete the transition in the future.

Electric vehicles (EVs) can be much more environmentally-responsible than gasoline powered vehicles, but their carbon footprint is coupled to how the electricity that charges them is produced. In some states with a heavy dependence on coal-fired power plants, my Prius would be more environmentally friendly. In states with a better mix of renewable energy on the grid, the better choice would be an EV. Obviously, charging at home with solar power or charging from a grid with a very high percentage of renewable energy would be the best choice.

My wife drives a Prius Prime, which runs as an EV for about thirty miles, then switches to hybrid mode. She is able to charge that car at home using some of our solar-generated electricity. This means she drives with a very small carbon footprint.

But don't think you have to purchase a new vehicle to improve your gas mileage. There are things you can do in any car to boost the efficiency. The first one is easy: keep your tires inflated to the proper pressure. When you need new tires, consider LRR tires—they will help any vehicle. Just looking ahead can boost mileage. If you can anticipate upcoming slowdowns or stops, you can coast for a while before applying the brakes. On a road with many traffic signals, always look ahead before you blast down the street only to have to stop again a short distance later. And just because your car can accelerate quickly doesn't mean you have to do it. The slow and steady tortoise analogy definitely wins the efficiency award, and often arrives just as fast.

Reducing your transportation energy use benefits you directly. If many of us reduce our transportation energy, there is a large benefit to society. Over the past decade, if we had all made choices to cut our transportation fuel use in half, it would have either eliminated almost all oil imports or significantly reduced the amount of drilling and fracking in the United States. This would have resulted in less water consumption and a reduction in air and water pollution. It would have also resulted in a reduction in fuel prices due to drastic demand reduction. Sadly, lower fuel prices often drive people to make poor fuel economy decisions during their vehicle purchases, so efficiency in transportation needs to be a constant effort.

Food Finance

This may come as a surprise to some, but you can actually cook food at home. When I was growing up, we ate out at a restaurant only on vacation and maybe twice a year near our home. Now, there seem to be more restaurants than homes, and they are usually quite busy. I can go to the grocery store and buy enough ingredients to eat well at home for a week for the price of just a couple of meals at a restaurant. And the home-cooked meals are generally more nutritious with a lower calorie count.

I've finally started doing some gardening. It's pretty efficient to walk outside and pluck some lettuce and tomatoes out of the garden for a nice salad. I'm not anywhere near self-sufficient, though, as I'm in the early, modest, trial-and-error stage. But that's how most good things start. There aren't many people who are just naturally experts at something. You have to try, sometimes fail, and keep learning and growing. In the case of gardening, you just have to get your hands dirty—literally. A community garden is more of an integrated approach. If you have neighbors with gardening skills and knowledge, you can supply labor, supplies, etc., while you learn, and you can all benefit from the produce. Converting many of the pampered home turf areas to productive gardens would be a great step. Instead of watering and fertilizing a lawn, which you then choose to mow and trim, you can harvest home-grown organic food.

You can optimize your food purchases, too. Buying some high-use items in bulk can save money. I rarely look at the overall price of items, but instead check the unit price. The largest bottle of ketchup doesn't always have the lowest unit price. You can't assume; you need to take a moment and look. However, you also must consider a larger portion can help reduce packaging waste.

I purchase organic products when possible. Many people assume organic food is somehow more nutritious. It's not. The benefit of organic food comes from several connected factors. One is consumers' reduced exposure to pesticides and herbicides. Avoiding that exposure means organic is a healthier choice. Another benefit is to the farm workers, whose exposure to pesticides and herbicides is also reduced, and farm workers are exposed at much higher levels than consumers. Don't forget that these workers' illnesses impact the cost of healthcare for everyone. Another benefit is to the environment. Eliminating herbicides helps reduce the spread of herbicide-resistant plants. Those plants lead to even stronger and more dangerous products in an endless and losing war against nature. The same cycle applies for pesticides. Species develop resistance, and then companies develop and sell even harsher chemicals that we get exposed to. Herbicides and pesticides are not very selective and kill many beneficial plants, animals, and organisms. Conventional farming uses fertilizers with high nitrogen content. Some of this runs off into rivers and collects in lakes and larger bodies of water. This nitrogen produces algae blooms and results in fish (and other aquatic life) kills and even large "dead zones" in the Gulf of Mexico. Organic farming has many benefits to you and society.

The same logic applies to meat that has not been doped with antibiotics or hormones. Overuse of antibiotics in our food chain has led to more antibiotic-resistant bacteria. In 2016, I saw the most ludicrous TV commercial over and over again that claimed "raised without antibiotics" was a marketing scam. It was from one of the large chicken-processing companies, and their claim was that, by law, chickens had to be free of antibiotics when they left the farm. They implied anyone claiming their chickens were raised without antibiotics was just performing a marketing stunt. In their minds, it was okay to overuse antibiotics, which leads to a dangerous increase in antibiotic resistance, as long as they cut back on the dosage before the chickens were processed. They are missing the point and deceiving people. Worst of all, the commercial said "raised without antibiotics" was just a marketing gimmick, then showed their product with the label "100% Natural"—a big marketing gimmick. You know what else is natural? Arsenic, but you probably shouldn't ingest a bunch of it. Their marketing campaign led me to avoid their product completely. See the next section for more about marketing resistance.

Marketing Immunity

This might be one of the most important sections of this book. I was apparently born with some type of marketing immunity. If you don't have this, you should develop it. Ignore marketing. It's mostly for things you will never need, but the campaign is designed to make you want it or even think you need it. Being able to distinguish wants from needs is a big part of good financial strategy. It's okay to indulge in a few wants—but only after the needs and the savings goals have been met. Then, if you can continue to defer the wants, you'll be in better financial shape to purchase some much nicer wants in the future. It's called delayed gratification, and there are many studies that show successful people practice it from a very young age. Look up the Stanford Marshmallow Experiment to see how children who had some self-control and waited for a better reward were far more successful in later life. Before you lament you might not have been born that way, other studies have shown the behavior can be modified. Once you practice it in one area and achieve some success, it becomes easier to apply delayed gratification to all parts of your life.

I wasn't completely immune to marketing as a child, but I received a great vaccination when I became a teenager. My grandmother gave me a $100 bill when I turned thirteen. This was in 1973, so that's equivalent to $570 in 2018 dollars. That's a lot of money for a thirteen-year-old kid. Video games had just started appearing, and I saw an advertisement for the Magnavox Odyssey Video Game System that hooked up to your home TV set. On the TV commercial, they were playing all sorts of games with different-colored graphic screens. And I wanted it. I really, really wanted it. And it happened to cost $100. I went to the store, and, without even reading the fine print on the box, I fell for the colorful graphics shown on the box cover and spent my $100. They only had one left on the shelf, which made it seem that much more urgent. It was one of the few times marketing sucked me right in.

When I returned home and pulled it out of the box, it was just a controller that hooked up to the TV so you could move dots around., The fancy graphics consisted of plastic overlays that stuck to the TV screen via static electricity. It was not a good purchase. And I still remember that lesson to this day. I never make an impulse buy. If there is something I want, then I will at least sleep on the idea overnight—and generally I'll wait much longer. I'll start researching it, which gives me more data and more time to make a better decision. More often than not, this leads me to NOT buy something. If it turns out I really did need that item, it will become self-evident and I can buy it later. That Odyssey box was when I got my Ph.D. in anti-marketing. If I could invent a drug, it would be one that insulated people from marketing—especially, and ironically, from the prescription drug marketing on TV.

I already mentioned the deceptive advertisement about antibiotics in chickens. You should be very skeptical of all corporate marketing efforts, especially the subtle ones with product placement and sponsorships. I understand they want to get their name in front of you, which is fine, but don't purchase anything based on their claims. Research first.

And why do many people pay extra money to walk around like a billboard promoting a specific name brand? I understand if you are paying for legitimate quality, but often people pay extra just for a specific brand or logo when there is no discernable difference between the branded product and a lower cost competitor. Companies should pay you to advertise their products, not the reverse.

Part of the problem is our search for simple solutions. A pill to fix this, a purchase to make us feel better about ourselves, a fancy outfit to try and impress someone. Instead of complaining about the price of prescription drugs, figure out a way to get off them. Yes, I agree drug prices are outrageous, and I do understand some people need medication. However, I would bet a large percentage of prescription drugs and over-the-counter drugs are not needed, and in fact are probably more harmful than helpful. If they were actually curing your issue, why would you need to keep refilling the prescription? It's an old tale, but if you are having issues, you should keep doing root cause analysis until you figure out the root of the problem. Popping a pill might seem easier than lifestyle changes, but the pill is not treating the cause of the problem, only the symptoms—and sometimes not even very well.

Political Marketing

Since I'm writing this after the 2016 U.S. election, speaking of being skeptical about marketing... What the heck, people? I mentioned finding unbiased sources of information and data you can use to make the best choice for a product. The same thing applies to choosing a candidate for office. You have to filter through the noise and get down to solid information—and that requires some work on your part. The harder someone is trying to feed you something, the more you should just close your mouth. One, so you don't ingest it, and two, so you don't repeat it. (And now I'm starting to think about dropping out of society yet again.) The use of false fear tactics is the worst trick and should be skeptically reviewed and in no way rewarded with your vote.

I often think about politicians from a financial standpoint. The candidates who raise most of their money from a few sources, especially PACs, would seem to be more beholden to a few people. Candidates who raise most of their money from small donations, from many people, would seem to have the interest of the general public in mind.

The harder someone is trying to feed you something,
the more you should just close your mouth.
One, so you don't ingest it, and two, so you don't repeat it.

There are several well-known steps that could make our selection of government fairer and more efficient, but some in power are not as interested in being fair and efficient as they are in getting re-elected. Non-gerrymandered districts, election finance reform, easy voter registration, extended early voting options, and voting on a weekend (or make voting day a holiday) are just a few steps to improve the democratic process. The entire system could be much more efficient, which would encourage more people to participate.

The influence of big money, and the marketing it provides, is probably the biggest impediment to a fair and honest electoral process. If everyone applied researched and rigorous selection criteria to decide who received their vote, it could help solve a lot of the other challenges we are facing.

Gift Giving

It's not a law that you have to give gifts at holidays. This is especially true during the frenzied gift stampede in the last six weeks of the year. People sometimes stretch their finances and place too much stress on themselves trying for some perceived perfection. Often, the gift isn't even something that's needed or appreciated. I spent many years telling people I didn't want any gifts, but most of the time they ignored me. But I was serious. I would much rather do my research and get the right thing at the right price instead of having someone give me something I can't use. Most people have too much "stuff" already. Before you start calling me Scrooge or the Grinch, let me note a better way. Be opportunistic. Don't give gifts because a calendar and a thousand ads tell you to. Give a gift when the perfect opportunity arises and you can help someone. It can be done on any day or any year. It can be an item they need, or an experience. The element of surprise will make it extra special.

Health and Leisure

Efficient Vacations

When I take a vacation, I essentially get a two-for-one deal. I get to experience the destination twice—once while researching it, and once in person enjoying it. My vacation-planning spreadsheets are sometimes judged as rigid and overdone. But anyone who has travelled with me can attest I can fit more fun into a vacation day than anyone else, and do so very cost-effectively.

I start by researching an area using the many travel sites available. I begin to generate a list of things we want to do and see. After assembling the major destinations, I use mapping tools to determine the optimal routing. I then start assembling a day-by-day plan. Once the daily plan has been generated, I go back to the travel sites to narrow down a top list of lodging options. I then use price-searching tools to find the best deal on places we want to stay. Like most choices I make, I rarely choose by price. I may use a price window for the search, but I find places we would like, then search for the best value.

Finally, I'll add data to the spreadsheet, such as sunrise, sunset, moonrise, and average temperatures (replaced by forecast temperature right before we depart). The weather data make efficient packing easier. The other data help refine the daily planning and let us know if it might be a nice night for a moonlit walk or for stargazing. I add all the addresses, phone numbers, confirmation numbers, and costs to this sheet as well, so everything we need is in a compact and portable form. It's printed (double sided, of course) and placed on Dropbox for electronic sharing and backup. Table 3 is a segment of one of my travel spreadsheets.

This may seem rigid, but I'll build in some slack time in case we find something unexpected along the way or want to spend a little more time somewhere.

Planning vacations is quite enjoyable. I learn a lot about the places we are going to visit in advance. Then, while there, I can relax and enjoy everything a bit more. Some people have told me a lot of time on their vacations is spent trying to decide what they want to do next, then figuring out how to get there, where to park, where to eat, etc. Planning most of those activities in advance is the solution. I took a trip with a friend a few years ago, and she was amazed at how much we were able to see and do. The previous month she had been traveling with a group, and she said they spent most of their days trying to figure out what they were going to do that day. Consequently, they didn't get to do much.

Table 3. Sample vacation spreadsheet segment

Badlands, Devils Tower Trip			May 2018
Sat,May-26	293	Fly to Bismark, ND (BIS) - Drive to Badlands	62F-91F, Sunset 8:19pm; Moonrise 5:23pm
CDT			
10:45am		Depart for DFW airport	
11:45am		Parking / Lunch at Airport	
1:00pm		AA#5849 1:00p DFW - 3:41p BIS	RecLoc: XYZXYZ (used miles), 14A
12:15pm		AA#5849 1:00p DFW - 3:41p BIS	RecLoc: ABCXYZ (used miles), 14C
3:41pm		Arrive BIS	
4:00pm		Car Rental - Intermediate at Avis	Avis res: 12345678US2
CDT		Groceries / Dinner	Dan's Supermarket - 835 S. Washington St.
4:30pm	293 mi	Depart for Wall, SD - 5 hour drive	Dinner Stop - TBD
9:00pm		Arrive Wall, SD (gain hour)	
MDT-1		Super 8 In Wall, King, Micro/Fridge/Bkfst	Conf: 87654321
		711 Glenn St Wall, South Dakota 57790	605-279-2688
		Food: Badlands Saloon/Grill, Red Rock Restaurant, DQ, Subway	
Sun,May-27		Badlands National Park	62F-88F, Sun 5:12am - 8:20pm; Moon 6:26pm
MDT		Breakfast at hotel (included) / Pack Lunch	
30 min	25 mi	Badlands Loop Road - east	
		Prairie Homestead, NE Entrance, Big Badlands Overlook, Door Trail, Window Trail, Notch Trail, Chiff Shelf Trail	
	5 mi	Ben Reifel Visitors Center	
		Cedar Pass Area - Castle Trail, Medicine Root Trail	
	5 mi	Fossil Exhibit Trail, White River Valley, Big Foot Pass, Panorama Point, Prairie Winds, Burns Basin,	
	17 mi	Homestead, Conata Basin, Yellow Mounds, Ancient Hunters, Pinnacles	
	9 mi	to Hotel	
		Super 8 Wall	
		Food: Badlands Saloon/Grill, Red Rock Restaurant, DQ, Subway	

And no, we don't purchase vacation insurance. In all our decades of traveling it would have been used just once—for a weather delay in New Zealand. We were in Milford Sound. We had completed an overnight cruise and awoke to a fierce, early spring storm the next morning. The storm closed the road out of the sound due to downed trees and avalanche concerns. We spent an extra night there, but the next day they were still clearing the road, so we had to pay for a private sightseeing plane to fly us back to Queenstown in order to catch our next flight. The extra amount we spent for that weather-related event was far less than the decades of unused vacation insurance payments we would have made. Plus, it was a very scenic flight out.

I continue to hear U.S. citizens are not even taking all their earned vacation. If you optimize other areas of your life, you'll find the time and money to get away. And there is great value in traveling and spending time away from work. It's another area to find joy.

Efficient Exercise

The company I worked for was very progressive and built an on-site fitness center in the 1960s. This gym facilitated my commuting efficiency. I could drive in early and beat the traffic, go to the fitness center, get a shower, and be just minutes from my office. Or I could go after work and let the traffic settle. This on-site fitness center also hosted clubs for a variety of interests. Doing something is always easier when you have a group of like-minded people to do things with. For thirty years, I played basketball at 6:00 every Tuesday and Thursday morning. It was a good group. We played hard for the exercise, but often didn't even keep score. This kept fouling and arguments at a minimum. The spirit of fair and friendly competition attracted like-minded people to the mornings. I enjoyed going to hang out with the players, and accidentally got a lot of good exercise out of it.

We also had a running club, which formed the seed of a group that joined a national corporate track competition in 1979. I joined the team in 1983 and attended my first national meet in 1985. This team was a great motivator to work out, with the annual trip to the national meet serving as a nice carrot to dangle in front of us. I have run in every meet since 1985 and am still going at the time of this writing. I set an individual national record in the 200-meter sprint at age fifty, and I have run on three different relay teams that set national records.

Partly due to my eye for efficiency, I became team captain in 1998. Almost every event at the corporate meet is a relay or team-scoring event. At the meet, we have more than fifty team members competing in dozens of relay events that cover multiple age groups and distances. After a few years on the team, I began to understand all the events and began working to optimize our athlete placement. Studying past data and current performance levels allowed us to optimize all our races and improved our team score. Our long-time excellent coach, Rio King, trained people into peak shape, and I placed everyone in the right place. It all began with having the efficiency of having an on-site fitness facility.

Even our track practice workouts are time efficient. Rio recommends a set of drills that are done as a dynamic warmup. You are continuously moving during the drills, so it acts as aerobic conditioning at the same time. Once the drills are done you are warmed up, loose, and ready for an interval training workout.

I helped guide the team to twelve consecutive national championships starting in 2000. I was inducted into the United States Corporate Athletic Association Hall of Fame in 2002. Later that year, I got to carry the Olympic Torch as part of the 2002 torch relay for the Winter Olympics. Circling back to the difference that leadership can make, note that I didn't run track in high school. Although I demonstrated great quickness and speed in PE class, the coach told me I could only run on the track team if I quit band. I offered to split days at afterschool practice between track and band, but he told me, "It's all or nothing, son." So, I stuck with band. The band director, by the way, would have been fine with my splitting practice days.

My other efficient fitness strategy is pretty simple: incorporate activity into your day. Always take the stairs instead of the elevator. Park farther out and make your walk a little longer. Get a dog—they'll always remind you that you should be out walking. Especially now that I'm retired, I much prefer finding ways to exercise around the house instead of having to pack up stuff and drive to a gym or class. I can be finished before others even arrive. If you need some motivation, find a neighbor to walk, run, or bike with so you can motivate each other.

Efficient Wardrobe

I'm not as good at this as Mark Zuckerberg, who apparently purchases grey t-shirts and hoodies in bulk and wears them every day. That simple strategy removes the need to decide what to wear; just grab and go.

One efficiency I've embraced is not buying anything that needs to be dry cleaned. It's time-efficient because it eliminates additional trips. It's certainly cost-efficient, as people with clothes that need to be dry cleaned eventually spend more money cleaning them than they did purchasing them. It's also good for the environment to reduce or eliminate dry cleaning, as the process can be a major source of pollution.

My strategy is to maximize longevity. I have managed to keep the same weight for decades. (I've kept the same height as well, but that didn't require any action on my part.) My very old clothes still fit, so I buy very few new items each year. Some years, I've only replaced socks and underwear. I still have a shirt I bought in 1973, when I was 12. It was a bit big then, but it fits now.

For shoes, I wear only black running shoes—everywhere. I can work out in them or wear them with a format outfit. In fact, I got married in black running shoes. They are very comfortable, and I only need a couple of pair at a time. Once I found a brand that fit my feet well, I just stuck with it. Unfortunately, the marketing people make manufacturers update shoes every year. I would love for them to just keep making the same shoe that I really like year after year, but their game is to constantly make you think there is something new and better—even if they made it worse.

Societal Efficiency

These efficiency rewards are available in so many areas of our lives. And the real power is in the multiplying effect. If there are only a few people who embrace efficiency, the societal impact will be negligible. If many people embrace it, then positive and lasting change begins to occur. Our economy is consumer-driven, and it will only be a strong and lasting economy if we collectively make good choices.

As an example, our U.S. healthcare system is loaded with inefficiency and sub-optimized solutions. It's difficult to tackle such a large and complex system from a whole system perspective, but it's not impossible—and that's probably the only way to salvage such an out-of-control system. With each passing year, it becomes more necessary. The current path is unsustainable. We, as the consumers, have to be knowledgeable and demand changes.

Government

I want an optimized government. Unfortunately, every campaign and politician seem to run on a series of suboptimized solutions—special interest items that increase complexity and don't address the issues at their source. If I were running for office, my *Joy of Efficiency* platform would be quite different from anything you've seen or heard.

There will be differences of opinion about what roles the government should have, but as long as government has any role, I hope we can all agree it should be performed as efficiently and effectively as possible.

Tax Code

Tax policy is the power source for all politicians. The ability to grant favors and support specific items via the tax code is how we ended up with a bloated, complex system that no one understands. The IRS is not to blame—the string of elected officials, some with good intentions, have piled on over the years and created a monster.

The resulting complex tax code is where the cheats and scoundrels thrive. We've heard many suboptimal solutions. Talk of simplification usually takes the form of bracket simplification. For radical efficiency that neuters lobbyists and special interests, we need radical simplification of the tax code. Let's start by making it as simple as possible. No deductions or tax credits. Before you recoil at the loss of your favorite credit or deduction, remember to look at the overall picture. If all of them are eliminated and all income is counted the same, then we can raise the same revenue with a lower tax rate. And a progressive income tax rate is a small complexity that needs to be added, because most other taxes are regressive.

Here's the income tax form I dream about:

A. Enter your total annual income from all sources: _____
B. Subtract the poverty-level income (PLI): _____ (updated annually)
C. Your taxable income: _____

In my dream system, tax rates would be progressive and indexed to the poverty-level income, and the rates would be determined by the budget Congress passes, plus a few extra percent points to slowly reduce the national debt. The debt doesn't have to go to zero, but it does need to stay manageable. If Congress increases spending, then the rates automatically go up for the next budget year. If government spending is reduced, then the rates go down.

Cutting taxes without cutting spending is how the annual deficit and growing debt were created. The one thing worse than tax-and-spend is borrow-and-spend. If leaders want to cut tax rates, they have to cut spending first. If a spending increase is deemed necessary, then the case needs to be made for raising taxes. If we could couple the increase to where the money is honestly going, it would become a little easier to digest.

The annual adjustment factor would be published and linked to the budget. It should make people pay attention to the budget process, because they'll either pay for it or benefit from national fiscal discipline. If someone files a spending bill, they will also have to identify the funding to come from a cut in another area or advertise how much the additional spending will increase the tax rates.

That's it. There are no deductions or credits. No favors for anyone to buy. If you want to have a large family, that's your decision, but others don't have to subsidize you. If you want to give to charity, then good for you—but don't expect a tax subsidy. If you have mortgage interest, then congratulations—you own a house, but it shouldn't be subsidized. If you need a truck for your business, then that's part of your cost of doing business and should be reflected in your pricing. Capital gains and dividends are just another form of income—the fact that we currently tax them at a lower rate than actual labor is baffling. Stop it all, and we will greatly reduce the power that politicians wield over your life, and sometimes your freedom.

If we could do this, we could slice a big piece of corruption out of our political system. People pay a lot of money to our representatives for access so they can gain more than they pay through the system. This gain is usually delivered via the complex tax system. This simple tax plan stops one path of corruption in its tracks. The takers will move to the budget process and it will need close scrutiny, but corruption will be easier to stop than it currently is.

When you couple the tax rate to spending, you have near real-time feedback. Now, imagine the IRS shrinking dramatically, as fewer scoundrels will be able to hide in the complexity. The remaining IRS officials can go after those who are still cheating us all and hiding income.

As an added bonus, you can free up time and money you would have spent filling out, or paying someone to fill out, enormous tax forms. The current system always leaves you wondering if you missed some credit or deduction you could have taken. What about all those employees working in the tax industry? They can put their skills to use for something that adds value, like helping people learn about good money management.

If you think this tax proposal is too simple and would never work, then just ask yourself how well the current system works. It works for the takers and abusers, but only frustrates and burdens the rest of us. And the takers I'm calling out are not those struggling to get by using food stamps. The takers are the wealthy and greedy who just can't seem to get enough money and power. The complex tax code is their burglary tool of choice. We imprison those who steal from one person, but we let those who steal from all of us off the hook— or we give them a taxpayer bailout or elect them to office. When we equate having a lot of money with being successful, we're in trouble as a society. And we are in trouble now.

Building Design and Operation

Design Process

"Everything is designed. Few things are designed well." —Brian Reed

Great efficiency doesn't come about by accident. It comes about through attention to detail and excellent design.

Nothing lasts longer than poor design. Something that's poorly designed can bother you for many, many years. Poor design usually results from a bad design process. The integrative design process, also called integrated design, addresses the way we approach design. Building design has become very compartmentalized and linear. The current process has specialist after specialist contributing their expertise in a serial manner. The specialists might even optimize their portion of the design. Too often, though, these suboptimizations don't consider or optimize the entire design. That's what should be optimized—the whole system, the finished product. Having the best seats in an otherwise terrible car is not the goal. Designing a very efficient air conditioning system for an inefficient and leaky building is an example of a suboptimized process.

Instead of passing the design documents from expert to expert, the integrative design process brings all these experts together to share their talents and optimize the finished product as a whole. The key is to get everyone involved as early as possible. If we could improve our design processes across industries, then we could significantly improve the quality of many products for no additional cost, or possibly even a lower initial cost. The process is the key.

Take a small building project as an example. The usual path is for an architect to draw up the plans, then a civil engineer designs the structure and slab, then a mechanical engineer designs the air conditioning and plumbing systems, then an electrical engineer designs the power and lighting. Sometimes these disciplines never even meet. The plans get passed along and each specialist has to compensate for some issue. Maybe the design didn't leave enough room for proper duct sizing, or the daylighting is poor, requiring extra light fixtures, or there is a large wall of west-facing glass that causes the air conditioning to be much larger and more expensive to purchase and operate—and requires even larger ducts, for which there is no room.

In contrast, the integrative design process gets everyone together several times during the early design phase so they can identify and find solutions for all these issues together. This process results in a better design that's often easier, faster, and less expensive to build. It's also less expensive to operate. I used a building as an example, but this concept applies to almost anything we design and build. The designer of a toilet would benefit from the input of an experienced plumber who has installed and repaired hundreds of toilets. City planners would do a better job if they had a variety of voices providing input. And they would do even better if they brought those voices together to recognize common values and optimize the entire plan. Sometimes the best ideas come from the quietest voices. And if those voices aren't speaking up, you need to ask them—and listen.

In many cases, a poor design outcome is the result of not properly identifying the actual issue that needs to be addressed. The person in charge of a large power company might tell the design team they need to design an affordable way to distribute wires to the homes in a developing nation. Many hours will be devoted to solving that task. There may indeed be good ideas, and a good design might emerge. But they forgot to ask the fundamental question from the end-user standpoint. Do the people there want wires, or do they want electricity? Chances are they want affordable electricity. What if the most economical solution was not a central power plant with wires strung around the country, but a collection of distributed renewable energy systems with storage connected by a microgrid? Framing the design issue around the old way of thinking about electrical distribution might have eliminated the most elegant. Before convening a team, make sure the design goal is framed around solving the root issue.

Figure 4 depicts the integrative and iterative design process. The initial concept meeting should have as many people involved as possible—even those who don't have any work to do until near the end of construction. Their input is valuable. After a rough concept has been sketched out, there should be time allowed for all the disciplines to retreat for some detailed analysis and study. When everyone reunites for the schematic design, they can refine the earlier ideas and fit the pieces of the puzzle together. Then there is one more opportunity for the disciplines to refine their design, materials, numbers, costs, and other issues. One final design development session pulls it all together before the construction documents are prepared. The design development period is the best place to identify potential issues. It's much less expensive to revise something on paper than it is to change something in the field during construction.

Integrative Design Process: Loops

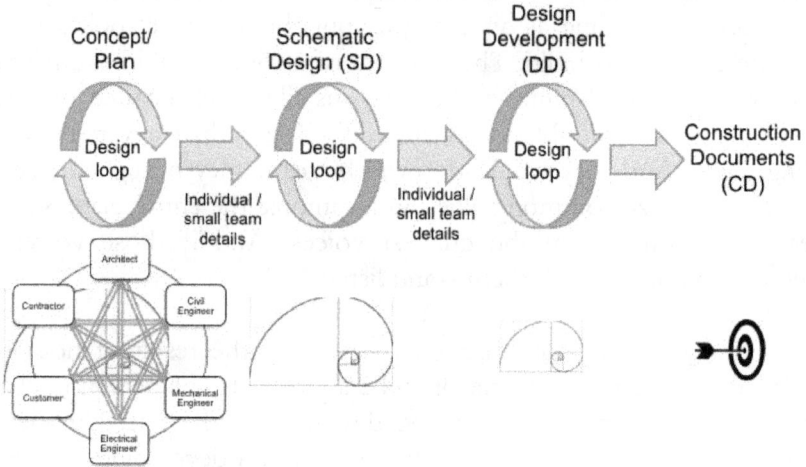

Figure 4. Integrative design loops

People often idolize the wrong type of model, such as a fashion model. Energy models are the real stars. Energy models use the design information to model the building's likely energy use. The model uses local typical hourly weather data over an entire year to estimate energy consumption. There should always be an energy model completed by the schematic design stage of a building project. Once a baseline model has been built, it's easy to change parameters (more insulation, better windows, etc.) and observe their impact on energy use. The energy model can help you choose the most cost-effective paths to pursue. It can also help you combine a suite of improvements to realize some very large savings. Sometimes it's the combination of many small items that lead to these breakthrough savings, such as improving the house shell so much you eliminate the need for air conditioning.

Improving the process of design is one of the most powerful tools we have to improve many aspects of our lives.

Energy Basics

Energy and Power: Electricity

When I think of efficiency, the first thing I think of is energy. Energy is so fundamental to everything, it *should* be a primary focus. Energy efficiency often cascades efficiency into many other areas.

Before we cover energy efficiency for a building, it would be best to define a few common terms. For electricity, there are two terms that are important to understand. First is **power**, which is measured in watts (W). Appliances and light bulbs will be listed at a certain wattage. If it's large, this number will be in kilowatts (kW), which is 1,000 watts. This is the amount of power required.

Energy is power over a period of time. If you run a one kW appliance for one hour, then you will consume one kilowatt-hour of energy (1kWh). This is what the electric meter on the side of the house measures—and what you pay for.

Power = watts or kilowatts
Energy = power x time = watt-hours or kilowatt-hours

If you had an 1,800 W appliance you ran for only five hours per month, it would use 9kWh of energy. If you had an old 100 W light bulb that you left on for twelve hours each night, it would use 36kWh of energy in a month.

Electricity is generally priced by the kWh. If you paid ten cents ($0.10) per kWh, then the appliance that used 9kWh would have cost you $0.90 for the month, while the light that used 36kWh would have cost $3.60.

Some utilities charge higher rates during peak-use times, and/or lower rates during low-use periods. People with electric vehicles or other large loads that can be scheduled at certain times should be aware of their local rate structure. Commercial and industrial users also have to manage a demand charge, which is essentially a peak-use fee. A demand charge is based on your highest kW power draw during a certain period, and you can lower it by managing your peak demand spikes.

About 75% of our electricity use in the U.S. goes to our buildings. By contrast, about 75% of our oil use goes to transportation: cars, buses, planes. Almost no electricity is produced from oil; instead, it is produced using coal, natural gas, nuclear, and renewables. The balance of oil and electricity consumed in the U.S. goes to industrial uses. Figure 5 illustrates the differences. Much more information on the subject can be found in *Reinventing Fire* (https://www.rmi.org/insight/reinventing-fire/).

Oil Use vs Electricity Use

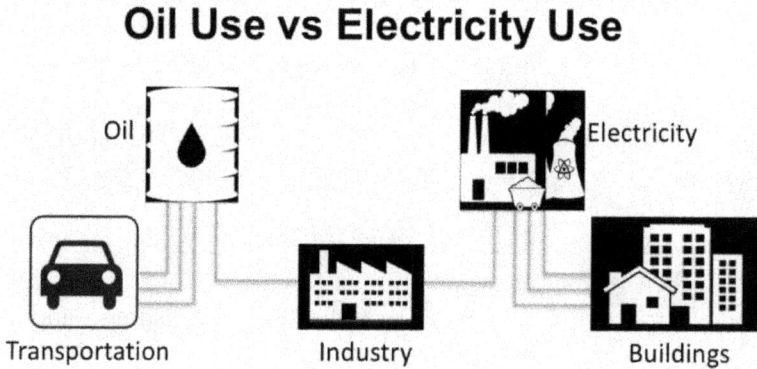

Figure 5. Oil use versus electricity use

Cooling and Heating Loads

Before you start picking cabinets and paint colors for a new house, let's pause and look at what drives heating and cooling in a home. There are two sources of residential energy impact (loads)—internal and external. External loads come from the weather and direct sunlight entering the windows or heating external surfaces that transfer heat into the building. Internal loads come from appliances and people in the house that emit heat. An old-fashioned incandescent light bulb is actually a small space heater, converting most of the energy it consumes into heat–with a little light as a byproduct.

Heat moves in three main ways: conduction, convection, and radiation. Heat moving through a solid surface is **conduction**. Your windows, walls, and roof will conduct heat into and out of your home. If the sun is shining on a brick wall, the heat will slowly conduct from the sunny exterior side to the interior side. The heat moves through different materials at different rates. The term **R-value** refers to the level of resistance a material offers to moving heat. A high R-value material will move heat less readily than a low R-value material.

Convection involves air movement. If you have an air space between things (like between two panes of glass), then air movement can accelerate the rate of heat transfer between those surfaces. Convection also occurs when the wind blows along the side of a wall, modifying the energy transfer of the wall beyond its simple conduction. Therefore, convection can impact the effective R-value of a material.

Radiation is the least understood of the heat transfer mechanisms. A simple campfire analogy (Figure 6) is one way to explain. If you are outside on a cold night with a large campfire, you can feel the heat on your face as you approach the fire. The fire is indeed transferring some heat to the surrounding air, but the air next to your face is still cold—yet you feel intense heat on your face. That heat is radiating from the warm body (fire) to the cooler body (you). It's not heating the air around you, it's radiating the heat to you. This is infrared, radiant heat. It's also the kind of heat you feel through the windows in your home.

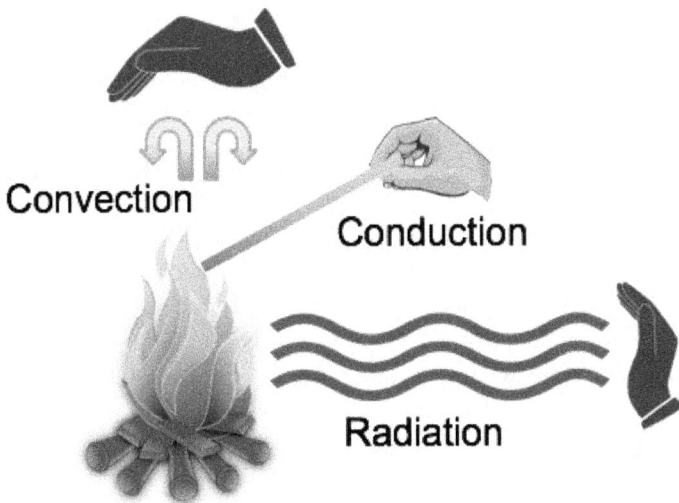

Figure 6. Conduction, convection, and radiation

While cooling loads are a mix of exterior and interior factors, heating loads primarily come from exterior factors: the weather and how well your house is protected from the elements. Improving insulation and reducing air infiltration (air leaks) will greatly reduce your heating load. Collecting free solar energy in the winter is also a good strategy.

In the U.S., we still measure thermal energy in British Thermal Units (Btu). One Btu is the amount of work needed to raise the temperature of one pound of water by one-degree Fahrenheit (°F). You will run across the term most often when discussing air conditioning or heating. One ton of cooling is equal to 12,000 Btus per hour. A three-ton air conditioning unit can produce 36,000 Btus of cooling in an hour.

In the metric system, one Btu equals 1.055 kilojoules. Converting to power and the more familiar watt is done using Btu/ hour. One watt is equivalent to 3.412 Btu/hour. Therefore, one ton of cooling (12,000 Btu/hour) is equivalent to 3.5 kW.

Cooling system efficiency for air conditioners or heat pumps is measured using a few different units. One is the Coefficient of Performance (COP). Another is the Energy Efficiency Ratio (EER). A third is the Seasonal Energy Efficiency Ratio (SEER). There is a European version, ESEER. Each measure has its value, but for shopping comparisons, SEER is probably used most often.

The COP is simply the useful heating or cooling provided divided by the work required to generate that heating or cooling. An efficient unit with a COP of 3.5 is providing 3.5 units of heating or cooling for every one unit of energy put in. But note the rating does not factor in the environmental conditions. Is it a mild day or a very hot or cold day? The COP can be measured at any condition, but it is likely to change as conditions change. The COP is unitless, as it simply divides energy (kW) by energy (kW).

The EER is similar to the COP, but it converts the numerator to Btu. For cooling, EER is generally calculated using a 95°F outside temperature, an inside temperature of 80°F, and 50% relative humidity.

The SEER uses the climate data across a typical weather year to provide a better indicator of how a unit will perform across a variety of conditions. In the U.S., building codes require a minimum SEER of 14 (as of 2015). There are units available that can perform at triple this minimum level.

Finally, there is often a balancing issue. In climates that require both heating and cooling, it's good to balance the heating and cooling load during the design. Not every energy-saving decision affects both the same. If you need more heating than cooling, you might consider improvements such as perimeter slab insulation, which reduces more heat loss than it prevents heat gain, especially in colder climates. If you need more cooling, then reduce direct solar gain or improve roof reflectivity. Unbalanced loads are most problematic if you use one unit, such as a heat pump, to handle both heating and cooling. If the heating load drives you to install a larger system than is needed for cooling, then your cooling system will be oversized. An air conditioner that is oversized for the cooling load will "short cycle," which means it will run for a short time, then shut off. It cools, but it doesn't have time to dehumidify the air. (Air conditioners remove moisture from the air by passing the air across a cold coil and condensing the moisture out, which is a big part of how they make you feel more comfortable.). The unit has to run long enough to move all the air in the house across the coil in order to reduce the humidity. If it turns on and off frequently, you end up with a cool, but clammy house. That's less comfortable than a cool and dry house.

Moisture

Your comfort is determined by much more than just the air temperature. Air temperature is important, but humidity is also a major factor. The weather forecasts often provide the relative humidity number, but I prefer to know the dew point. The dew point is the temperature at which dew would form. If you were in a warm climate with a 65°F dew point, you would see condensation forming on any surface that was cooler than 65°F. Yet another measurement is the "wet bulb" temperature, which refers to the measuring technique. These numbers can be graphed in a psychrometric chart, such as the one below, which offers a good illustration of the relationship among these parameters.

In the psychrometric chart below (Figure 7), I've outlined a general range for human comfort. The temperature and humidity level play an important role. There are more complex comfort charts that consider air movement (like that from a ceiling fan) and other factors. There are also psychrometric plots showing the typical climate data for specific locations. These can be useful in devising a cooling/heating strategy for your climate. You take the weather nature throws at you and devise the most efficient method to bring the indoor conditions into the comfort zone.

The red circle in Figure 7 shows a temperature of 72°F and a relative humidity of 50%. This is near the middle of the human comfort zone. The orange horizontal line is drawn from that point to the edge of the chart. Then you read vertically down to the temperature number, and that indicates the dew point. In this case, it is about 52°F. The blue line that slants up to the left indicates the wet bulb temperature where it intersects the edge of the chart, and extending it up further shows the enthalpy. In this case, the wet bulb temperature is just under 60°F and the enthalpy is just over 26 Btu/lb. of dry air. Enthalpy is used in thermal calculations to represent the energy content of the air. It's a bit more detail than most of you will need. The main point is the power of the psychrometric chart to visualize detail about the thermal conditions. As a bonus, psychrometric is a fun word to say.

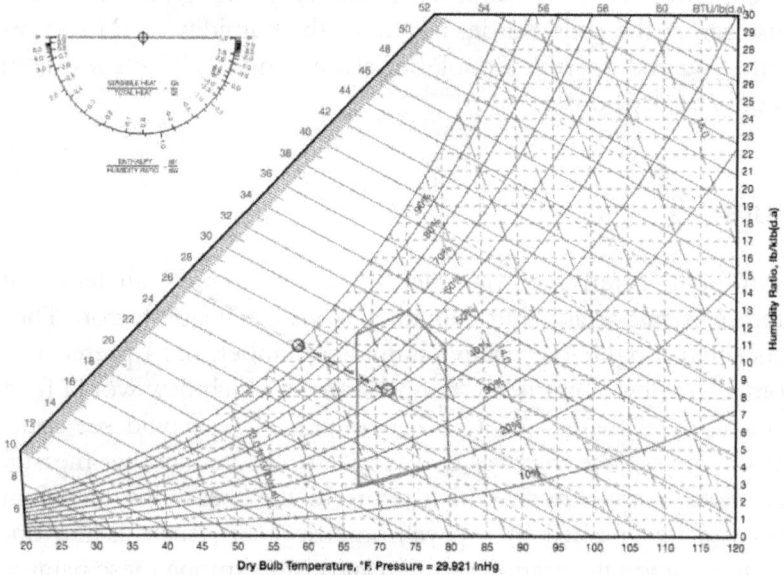

Figure 7. Psychrometric chart showing the human comfort zone

Understanding the dew point can help you keep your house comfortable. For example, during the spring and fall at our house, we use the dew point as a key indicator of whether we should open the windows or not. In our climate, if the dew point is below 60°F (15°C) and the temperature outside is cooler than inside, we open the windows for some free cooling. If the dew point is above 60°F, then the outside air would bring too much moisture into the house, so we'll run the air-conditioner instead.

Too low a dew point can make you uncomfortable, too. Your lips and skin will be dry. If you have a well-sealed house, you can generally keep the dew point in a comfortable range by trapping moisture from indoor water use such as showers.

As explained previously, an oversized cooling system will not adequately dehumidify the air in the house. The unit needs to run long enough to let the air pass across the cooling coil and condense out the moisture.

Efficient Home

For most of us, the largest expenditure we'll make in our lives is our house—both the acquisition and the upkeep. It's also the place where we spend the majority of our time, even if much of it is sleeping. Yet the home design and building industry has been slow to recognize the benefits of efficiency and simplicity. And they've been slow to recognize indoor air quality issues. Buyers and builders often prioritize superficial home trends over substantive items. If you are a developer, architect, or home builder, you should pay attention to these design tips—and embrace them. If you are a potential home buyer, you should check for these and walk away if too many of them have been ignored. Stop buying poorly designed homes if you want to drive change. I'll say it again: nothing lasts longer than poor design.

The smartest people sometimes build elegantly dumb houses, which is far superior to an overly complex, but inefficient, "smart home."

There has been a lot of buzz about smart homes. Generally, the term *smart home* is used for electronic products with communication features. My definition of a smart home is somewhat different: it should be a quality-built, energy-efficient, low-maintenance house. The smartest people sometimes build elegantly dumb houses—in a good way. And there is something to be said for simplicity. There's an old quote attributed to Albert Einstein that says, "Make things as simple as possible, but not simpler." Another quote, attributed to Village Homes developer Michael Corbett, that's good to remember: "You know you are on the right track when your solution for one problem accidentally solves several others."

In the sections below, you'll see the process and examples from designing my own house. My house design experience is primarily in a mixed climate at about 33 degrees latitude, near Dallas, Texas. This climate zone is primarily hot and humid, but we can get strong cold snaps in the winter and will get well below freezing several times each year. Passive solar in my area generally means rejecting solar heat for much of the year, though there are a few months where we can use it for space heating. The following sections will take you through our house-design process. I'll try to generalize in design principles, but remember, all good design is local and specific to your climate and location.

Here's the story of *The Westbrook House.* (Also see https://enerjazz.com/house)

The Land

The plot of land you build on is important. People often look for a convenient location, and perhaps good views, but there are many other things to consider as well. Orientation is covered in an upcoming section. Soil type is another issue. You want something that's going to be stable for your house foundation. If the land has native trees and grasses, and you are careful to preserve them, you won't need to landscape and irrigate much space, and you'll have hardy, well-adapted plants. Nature provides so many well-designed services for us—if we don't mess them up, intentionally or unintentionally.

The land we bought was a hidden gem. It was 2.2 acres (0.9 hectares) of land. It has thin soil, mostly weathered limestone near the surface, so it had never been farmed. Consequently, it had abundant native trees and grasses. These hardy, diverse trees and grasses had hundreds of years of natural selection going for them. We roped off all but a small staging and parking area to keep construction vehicles off the tree roots and the wildflower meadows. Preservation is much easier than restoration.

Finding this land required the perfect combination of the personality differences between my wife and me. My approach to things is calculated and methodical. Every Sunday I would scan the newspaper classified ads for land. For those young readers who grew up with the internet, this is how we used to do things—advertisements in the newspaper. I would look them up on a map (a paper map, as there were no online maps yet), then check the Collin County soil map to see what type of soil it was on. Much of the soil in North Texas is a thick black clay that shrinks and swells with the weather and creates foundation problems. I was searching for land in a rarer category, Edd2 (Eddy Gravelly Loam). After a while, I could tell by looking at the types of grasses and trees growing on the land what type of soil it had. I wanted Edd2 for the stable soil (important for a solid house foundation) and the diverse native plants that grew on it, as it was likely to have never been farmed.

We would make a list and map out a weekend drive to look at parcels. After one of these weekend excursions, we were driving back toward home, and not far from the property we had gone to see, we came to a little street intersecting the road we were driving on. There were a lot of trees along the street, and my wife said, "Turn down here." (My wife is more spontaneous than I am. On my own I would have probably not turned down that street. We make a good couple.)

And it was a magical street. Trees lining both sides opened to some hilly meadows and back to trees. The houses were scattered, and it was quite lovely. And then the strangest thing happened. My wife spotted a small sign on a tree that was almost covered by leaves. My wife doesn't have great vision; I'm usually the one spotting the hawk in the trees and anything else more than a few feet away. But she saw the sign. We got out and moved the leaves covering part of it to reveal a phone number. I checked it on the soil map, but I could already tell it was Edd2. We called after we returned home. The 88-year-old lawyer who had owned about 23 acres in the area had this 2.2-acre parcel for sale, but it was way out of my price range and well above the tax value. I thanked him for his time and went back to my search.

But this land kept calling me. Whenever I was out in the area looking at other parcels I would drive to this property, get out and walk around. After about six months I called the owner back and asked if he was ready to come down on his price. I found it odd he didn't have the property listed anywhere—just a sign on a tree that was covered with leaves for half the year. He didn't budge. I called again six months later. No movement. My wife was growing impatient and thought we would never get a parcel. But the standard had been set, and nothing else we looked at matched up to this one property.

Then, about six months after I had last called the owner, I visited in spring when the redbuds were in bloom, and I knew this was where we had to live. I called again. And this time the owner's wife answered. She said her husband had run to the store and would be back soon. I told her I was calling about the land in Fairview, and we started talking about it. By this point I knew most of the plants and trees growing there, and she did too. We made a connection with our appreciation of nature and talked about the various trees, grasses, wildflowers, and animals, and she said she would have her husband call me. A short while later the phone rang, and he dropped his price by 25%—and we bought it. My wife's theory is the owner's wife told her husband, "You need to sell that land to that nice young man who will take good care of the trees, plants, and animals."

The price still seemed high, but we decided we should take the chance. We had saved up and it was what we wanted (see the earlier section about financial efficiency). We bought the land with cash we had saved. The morning of the closing, my wife found out she was pregnant with our daughter. After we signed we immediately started saving again to build a house...and raise a child.

The only disturbed area of the property was right in the center, where the previous owner had built a chinchilla barn many years ago. It had fallen into a pile of decaying wood. I cleared the wood and small trees until I reached the large trees. I then measured the distance between the big native trees and designed the house to fit in that gap.

By not disturbing most of the land, we've reaped many long-term benefits. First, we didn't have to purchase many plants, just a few for the area right around the house. The trees and plants we have are very hardy. They are only here because they (or their plant parents) could survive the worst weather that has been thrown at them over hundreds of years. They've survived the worst drought and the extreme temperatures. They've fought off pests and disease and made it through wildfires—or regenerated after them. And because we left the forest intact, the trees can protect each other from wind. A forest always survives better than a single, lone tree. And the small trees are the future forest. Too many people trim up the trees and remove the small trees. Those small trees are the forest of the future.

We're rewarded with a variety of flowering trees and plants in the spring and by fabulous fall color in the winter. We don't need to irrigate because the plants have evolved to survive on what nature provides. We don't have to mow, edge, or trim the lawn. The only maintenance is some occasional tree trimming near the house and along the paths in the woods. And we have a natural zoo on our land. We even put up a trail camera to capture all the night life—possums, raccoons, armadillos, road runners, coyotes, bobcats, skunks, and even the occasional fox. We have owls, hawks, woodpeckers, cardinals, blue jays, bluebirds, and countless other birds.

House-Building Envelope

Orientation

Building orientation is usually not a topic of discussion, but it should be. If developers would simply lay out the majority of streets in an east-west direction, homes in that development could easily reduce their cooling and heating energy use by 30%. (Note I said the heating and cooling energy, not the entire house energy.) It's a big savings, since in our area heating and cooling can account for more than half of the typical utility bill. Orientation is important because most of the windows are usually on the front and rear of a building. If those windows face north and south (pole and equator), it's much easier to control unwanted solar gain in the hot months and to capture free solar energy in the cold months. If you are looking to purchase an existing house, bring a compass with you and see where most of the windows are. If they are on the east and west sides, then move on—and tell the builder why you aren't buying it.

When I see homes going up with a big bank of west-facing windows I always think I should start a window shading company, because you can almost guarantee during that first summer, when people are broiling in their home, they'll gladly pay someone to install solar screens or other shading devices on their windows. And sure enough, during that first summer I see all the solar screens being installed. This is a problem that could be avoided with a little thought when the development is being planned and houses designed. Developers should try to orient most of the streets east-west, which would minimize the east and west-facing windows on the homes.

Finding the right land and orienting your house properly are no-cost, high impact steps you can take to increase your comfort and lower your energy costs.

For those developing multiple houses, there is also an opportunity to reduce infrastructure distribution costs with clustering. Instead of spreading forty houses over forty one-acre lots, you can cluster the forty houses onto a smaller portion and leave a large section of open, green space. It could be forty homes on ¾ acre lots and a ten-acre open space. Clustering allows the developer to reduce the amount of infrastructure required. The roads, water lines, sewer lines, and other utility runs will be shorter. It also enables the developer to maintain the zoned net density—there are no additional homes, just differently arranged homes. The open space created can remain vacant or be used as a park. Homeowners also benefit from less property to maintain and pay taxes on, while they benefit from the shared open space. This type of development can leave more contiguous area in a natural state, which is better for plants, runoff absorption, air quality, wildlife, and people. It's the proverbial win-win.

Figure 8 depicts a compass. The compass has no communication ability or social media presence. The primary technology is a small magnet on a pivoting stick.

Figure 8. A compass

By intentionally facing your house in a certain direction, you can reduce your cooling/heating costs by about 30%. And it costs you nothing to do this. It's free. You just need good design—passive solar design.

Reader quiz:
The sun rises in the _____.
The sun sets in the _____.

"East" and "west" are the generally correct answers, but it is actually slightly more complicated due to the axial tilt of the earth. Around Christmas, when someone asks if you know the "reason for the season?" the clear and accurate answer is axial tilt. During summer in the northern hemisphere, the sun rises north of due east and sets north of due west (27 degrees north of due east/west here in Dallas, Texas). The sun also climbs very high in the sky at noon. In the winter, it rises to the south of due east and sets to the south of due west. It also peaks at a much lower point in the sky in the winter. Figure 9 indicates the sun pattern at my house.

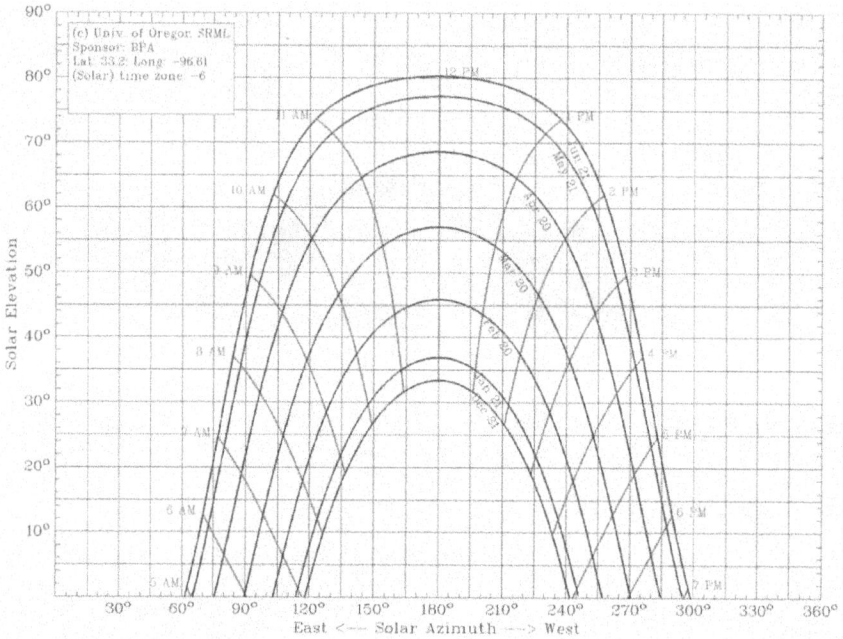

Figure 9. Sun path chart for Fairview, Texas

This is an unwavering annual pattern that can be used to your comfort and cost advantage by using what's called passive solar design.

If you orient the house with most windows on the equator side (south side in the northern hemisphere), and the fewest windows on the east and west, then you have used passive solar design. If you put some overhangs on the equator-facing windows so they provide shade from the high summer sun, but let the low winter sun into your home, then you have used passive solar design. Overhang sizing is quite simple and best expressed by Bart Simpson to Lisa while playing miniature golf: "I can't believe it, you've actually found a practical use for geometry!" The math is pretty simple for equator-facing window overhangs. If you want to keep the direct sun out of your window in the hotter months, then the angle between the wall and a line drawn from the base of the window to the edge of the overhang should equal your latitude. That will keep direct sun out between the equinoxes, which are around March 21st and September 21st). This is shown in Figure 10. The angle and overhang should be adjusted based on your climate. If you live in a cold climate and want a longer period of solar entry, you can reduce the angle and the overhang size. For the mixed climate we live in, the March and September equinoxes seemed to be good transition times.

Practical Use for Trigonometry

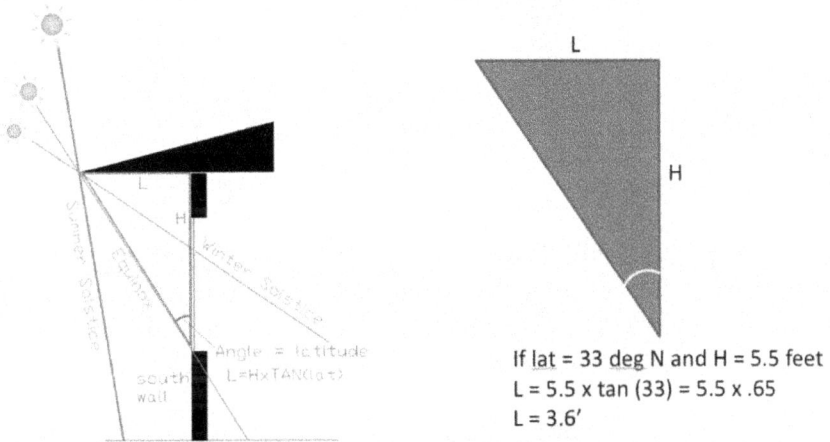

If lat = 33 deg N and H = 5.5 feet
L = 5.5 x tan (33) = 5.5 x .65
L = 3.6′

Figure 10. Window overhang design

Pole-facing (north-facing in the northern hemisphere) windows can provide soft daylighting with minimal unwanted heat gain during the summer. But windows do have lower insulation value than a wall, so balance the window counts carefully.

I need to stress passive solar design will have different goals and strategies depending on your location and climate. Most early passive solar projects, and books that were written about them, were for homes in cold climates, generally at elevation. Many of those had no need for cooling, just some heating in the winter. There was little research or information about passive solar for hot or even mixed climates. I had to create a Texas passive solar strategy. It should probably be called Passive Solar Rejection. Most of the year we strive to keep the solar heat out of the house. But our climate is mixed, and there are a few months where we would like to gather free heat from the sun into the house envelope. Shading and roof material become far more important factors in the warmer climate passive solar design.

We oriented the long face of our house about 13 degrees east of due south. Due south is ideal, but if you are within 15 degrees either way, you're close enough. We rotated ours slightly to fit between some large trees and provide slightly better view corridors.

There is little to no cost to orient a home properly and place windows thoughtfully, and large savings to be gained.

Building Shape

Once you get the orientation correct, the next important item is building shape. You want to maximize your usable floor area while minimizing your roof, slab, and wall area. This effort saves in both initial cost (less roof, concrete, brick, etc.) and long term operating cost (less exposed surface area to gain/lose heat).

Mathematically, a sphere might be the most efficient shape, but there are practical considerations, such as constructability, to deal with. (Also, you wouldn't want your sphere house breaking free and rolling down the street.) Unconventional shapes might be just as easy to build, but the issue is finding qualified and experienced people to do the work. Developing a quality supply chain and contractor network is vital to improving the way we currently design and build buildings.

Another goal of the shape is to maximize the equator and pole-facing wall surfaces while minimizing the east and west wall surfaces. Figure 11 shows several house layout designs and the effects of changes in wall, roof, and slab area. Minimizing exterior surfaces is the goal, though it has to be balanced with maximizing surfaces that face the equator. Equator-facing surfaces allow good control of light and heat gain. The data show a rectangle with the axis running east-west most likely provides the best balance of factors. A two-story plan works even better, as it reduces the amount of slab and roof area. Slabs and roofs are generally more expensive to build than walls, and the roof is where most unwanted heat gain enters the home.

Building Envelope Design

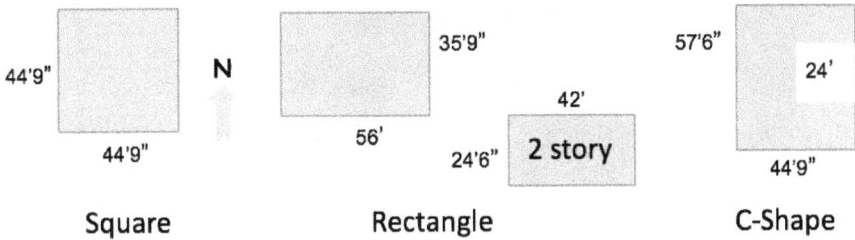

	Square	Rectangle	2 Story Rectangle	C-Shape	Goal
Floor Area (sf)	2,000	2,000	2,000	2,000	Same
Wall Area (sf)	1,432	1,468 (+3%)	2,261 (+58%)	2,020 (+41%)	Minimize
South Wall Area (sf)	358	448 (+25%)	714 (+99%)	358	Maximize
Roof or Slab Area	2,000	2,000	1,030 (-51%)	2,000	Minimize

The wrong shape increases initial cost and operating cost.

Figure 11. House shape comparison

In building our own house, we decided on a two-story rectangle for maximum efficiency of the majority of parameters, along with familiarity and ease of construction.

The shape is also important for utilizing natural daylighting. You want light without unwanted heat gain. Polar-facing windows will do this, as will equator-facing windows with proper overhangs. The only caution with equator-facing windows is you can get a LOT of light in the winter, and possibly some glare. There are techniques, such as light shelves, that can be used to project light deeper into the space while reducing glare.

Figure 12 shows how a light shelf can provide better distribution of light. The lower window is a view window. Exterior shading keeps direct sunlight from coming in. The upper window doesn't have any exterior shading, but the interior projection is a light shelf that reflects the light up and off the ceiling.

Figure 12. Light shelves

Because the sun's angle changes through the year, the equator-facing windows will receive a great variation in lighting. In summer, the high sun angle can combine with a properly sized overhang to eliminate any direct sun from entering the window. You'll still benefit from views and a good amount of softer natural lighting. In the winter, the low angle allows more direct sun in. This is good for heat gain, but might provide too much lighting. A little geometry with shade projections and light shelves can solve this issue.

House Size and Layout

We like big stuff, and I cannot lie. Big houses, big cars, big waistlines... At some point quantity became more valued than quality. We build houses way too large, and then we feel compelled to buy too much stuff to fill all that space.

> *We need a Goldilocks solution—not too small, not too large, but just right. We need the just-right house.*

House square footage has grown for decades, even as the average number of occupants has declined. More square footage means more cost to build, operate, and maintain. The tiny house movement has helped show people how a minimalist approach and clever design can let you live well in much less space. But tiny houses aren't for everyone. We need a Goldilocks solution—not too small, not too large, but just right. We need the *just-right* house.

Just Right House Size

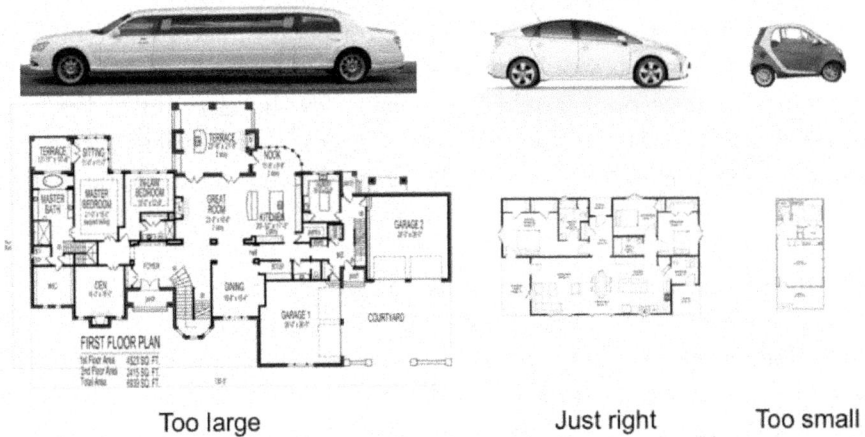

| Too large | Just right | Too small |

Figure 13. Just-right house size

To do this, you need to challenge your fantasies of how you think you'll use your house. I've seen people build extra bedrooms and baths for guests and then have them go completely unused. If you think about the extra cost to build, operate, and maintain the space—plus the additional property tax—you could put the occasional guest up at a really nice hotel and still have plenty of money left over. A flexible room for various uses, including occasional guests, might be a good compromise. In many houses, the formal dining room looks more like a museum than a place where people gather. Maybe that unused dining table could flip over and become a guest bed.

The cost of building too much space—one additional lightly-used bedroom:

Assume:	180 square feet (roughly 13x14 feet)
Initial cost:	$9,000–$27,000 (monthly payment on a mortgage = $500–$2000/yr.)
Additional furniture:	$1,500
Additional insurance:	$50–$100/yr.
Additional real estate tax:	$100–$500/yr.
Additional energy:	$10–$50/year
Additional maintenance (cleaning, window repair, roofing, flooring):	$20–80/year

At the low end of the scale, that extra bedroom will cost you almost $700/year. On average it would be closer to $1,700/year, and costs could be much higher. That amount would buy quite a few hotel room nights. If you still want the additional bedroom, make it a small and efficient space, and remember, if it's only for occasional use it doesn't need to be a typical bedroom size.

Identify the needed rooms and the approximate size of each, then work on the relationship of the rooms to each other. If possible, keep all the rooms with plumbing close together. This will minimize your capital cost (because you are purchasing less pipe) and shorten the wait time for hot water to get to a fixture. Prepare for the floorplan design to be a very iterative process as you play with various layouts until you get everything optimized. You have to balance many factors, but when you find the right solution it is an optimization, not a compromise. It's like working a complex jigsaw puzzle. It might take a while, but when you get it right you'll know it. Don't force-fit the pieces.

In our house, we wanted to keep the floorplan compact, so we went with a two-story design. In iterating the layout of the rooms, we discovered we could make the best fit by placing all the living areas upstairs and all the bedrooms on the ground floor. This is the exact opposite of most two-story homes—remember, everything is different at the Westbrook house. We thought about this design for a long time and decided there was no compelling reason not to choose the inverted floorplan. In fact, it had a couple of extra benefits. When we come in from the garage (we manage our accumulation of stuff well enough to actually park our cars in the garage), we are already on the level where we're going to drop most of our stuff and change clothes, and where the closets and laundry room are. After we change clothes, we head upstairs where we spend most of our waking hours. We have two outdoor decks off the second floor, so we still have access to the outdoors, and the half bath means our other needs are met without using the stairs. The other advantage is thermal. In a two-story house, the upper floor is usually about 3-4°F warmer, because heat naturally rises. I like it coolest when I sleep, so having our bedrooms on the lower floor provides cool air for slumber.

Figures 14 and 15 show our floor plans, and figure 16 provides a 3D look at the exterior so you can see how it's stacked for efficiency. Most windows on the south face with proper overhangs.

Westbrook House Ground Floor

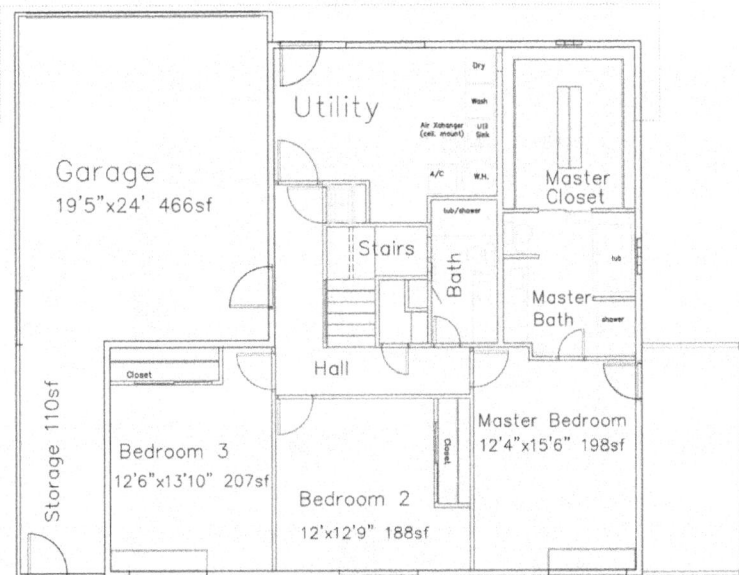

Figure 14. Westbrook House ground floor plan

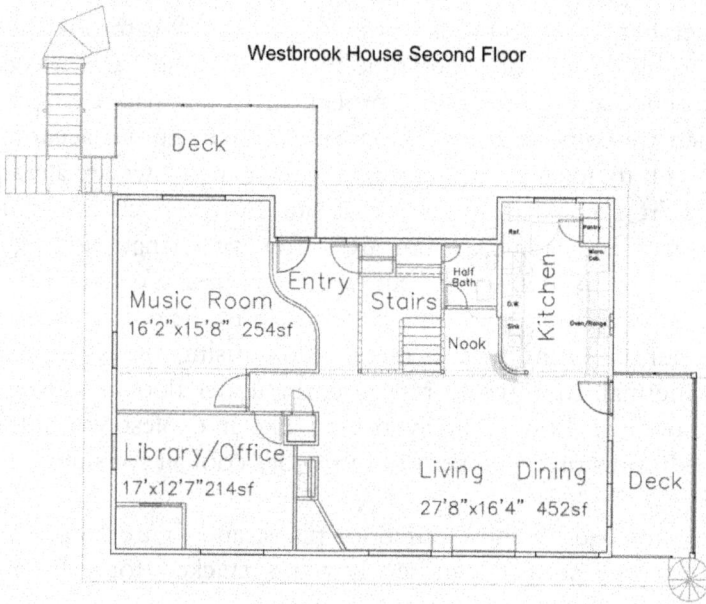

Westbrook House Second Floor

Figure 15. Westbrook House second floor plan

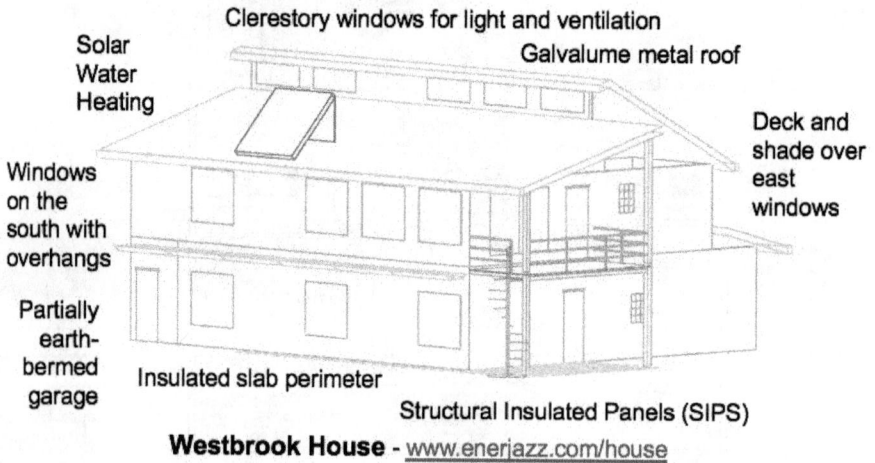

Compact, two story stacked

Clerestory windows for light and ventilation

Solar
Water
Heating

Galvalume metal roof

Deck and
shade over
east
windows

Windows
on the
south with
overhangs

Partially
earth-
bermed
garage

Insulated slab perimeter

Structural Insulated Panels (SIPS)

Westbrook House - www.enerjazz.com/house

Figure 16. Westbrook House 3D rendering

Attics

Most houses in Texas and the U.S. are built with attics. And usually those attics are designed or built poorly. Sometimes they don't have enough exit ventilation to let the hot air out. Often, builders will install several inefficient ventilation fans to try to exhaust the hot air, but the fans only succeed in raising your energy bill. When you move hot air out of an attic, replacement air has to come in from someplace. The replacement air should come in from soffit vents installed under the eaves, as illustrated in Figure 17. However, many builders don't install enough vents, or they allow attic insulation to block much of the air path. When air goes out the top of the attic, but there aren't enough incoming vents to provide adequate replacement air, the attic develops lower air pressure than the air-conditioned house below it. That negative pressure sucks the conditioned air up through gaps in the ceiling to replace the ventilation air. Then unconditioned outdoor air is drawn into the house through exterior gaps and cracks to replace your conditioned air.

To compound the problem, builders often place the air conditioning ducts and even the cooling unit itself in the attic. Placing the device that is working hard to produce cold air in the hottest location of the house is thermal suicide. The valuable chilled air is then distributed through poorly insulated, leaky ductwork to get it to the register which delivers it into your conditioned space. It's a senseless approach, but this is how most homes are built. Out of sight, out of mind—and some designers and builders are out of their minds for doing this.

Attic Issues

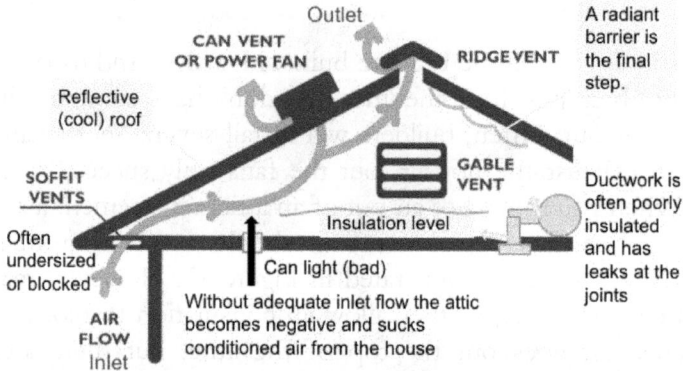

Figure 17. Typical attic ventilation and insulation issues and solutions

There are a few solutions to improve a poorly designed attic. If you ventilate the attic properly, that will help. That usually means adding additional inlet vents and making sure the vents you have aren't blocked by insulation. Another method is to insulate under the roof rafters rather than on top of the area above the ceiling, turning the attic into a semi-conditioned space. This works well and provides some additional space that is somewhat conditioned. It also allows your ducts and air conditioning equipment to operate in a less harsh environment.

Another option, which we chose, is not to build an attic. We used an offset shed roof design with a bank of equator -facing (south-facing) clerestory windows. These windows have several functions: they provide good natural daylighting, allow some solar heat gain in the winter, and are operable, which allows us to open them on mild nights, venting warm air out of the house and replacing it with cooler air from open windows on the lower floors. This illustrates my earlier statement that you know you are on the right track when your solution to one problem accidentally solves several others. Our inverted floor plan put our living areas on the second floor, where we could enjoy the spaciousness of the elevated ceiling. Having the high ceilings in a bedroom would have been a waste, since most of the time you are in the bedroom it's dark and your eyes are closed.

No attic was the best solution for us. You might ask, where do you store all your stuff when you don't have an attic? "Buy less stuff" is the answer.

Insulation and Infiltration

Figure 18 shows some examples of insulation. Insulation is inside your walls and ceiling (I hope), so you usually don't see it. It can be high quality or low quality. It can be installed well or poorly. It does not have WIFI, Bluetooth, ZigBee, Z-wave, Insteon, or X-10 communication abilities. It doesn't have an account with Facebook, Twitter, Instagram, Snapchat, Pinterest, or any other social media platform.

Yet insulation is one of the most important ways to keep your comfort high and operating costs low. It just sits there and works with no maintenance or input from you. But you have to install the right insulation properly. And if you are doing new construction, do not miss this critical opportunity.

Figure 18. Different types of insulation

R-value is a measure of how well heat conducts through a material. You can think of it as thermal resistance. A material with a low R-value will move heat quickly through it. A high R-value material will slow the transfer of energy and insulate you from exterior temperature changes. A wall's overall insulation value is a combination of the materials used in its construction. In the photo of the installer applying spray-on foam above, you can see wood studs spaced every 16" (41 cm). The insulation sprayed in the cavity might have an R-value of R-13 in a 3½" (9 cm) thickness—the thickness of a typical wood stud. However, those 1½" (3.8 cm) wide wood studs every 16" only have an R-value of about 3 or 4. When you add the bottom and top plates, the studs, the window, and door headers and blocking, the overall R-value of the assembly decreases dramatically. You might think you had an R-13 wall because that's the insulation value, but the composite performance is about an R-7 or 8. This phenomenon is called thermal bridging, where the studs conduct energy past the insulation. Oak Ridge National Laboratories has led the building industry in defining whole-wall R-value, an increasingly popular metric that tests the thermal resistance of an entire wall section. A 2×6 wall on 24" stud centers with R-19 fiberglass insulation turns out to provide an overall R-13.7 when considering the thermal bridging of the studs.

(Note that sometimes you will see the term U-value or U-factor. This is the inverse of R-value. A higher R-value is better, which means a lower U-value is better. Units of the U-value are $W/m^2\,^\circ C$ or Btu/hr-sq ft $^\circ F$.)

Insulation can reduce heat movement through building materials, but hot or cold air blowing through tiny gaps is like a car driving around a traffic barrier. That is called infiltration.

Figure 19 shows a tube of caulk in a caulk gun. Caulk is used to seal up cracks and air leaks. Like insulation, it has no communication ability or social media presence. It's slightly phallic, but not very sexy. Yet it's an important tool for stopping air infiltration.

Figure 19. Caulk

Building a "tight" house with minimal air leakage is an important way to keep your comfort high and your operating costs low. In addition to leaking energy, those air leaks are also the main path for dust, dirt, and bugs to enter your home. There are numerous infiltration-reduction products besides caulk, such as gaskets that go between the concrete slab and the bottom of your walls. There are boards and tapes that go on walls and around penetrations.

When you shop for a house, how much time do you spend checking out the insulation and airtightness of the structure? Do you know how to check the airtightness of your existing house?

Figure 20 is a picture of an excellent leak detector who will work for free. Spiders are very good at finding air leaks in your house. They will build a web near a leak because they know that potential food will be moving in and out of those leaks. We often repay them for their free leak-detection service by squashing them. Just plug the leaks and the spiders will move elsewhere.

Figure 20. Air-leak-detecting spider

If you aren't fond of spiders, then an energy auditor can perform a blower-door test on your house. A blower door is exactly what the name implies: a large fan placed in the doorway of your house, facing out, and sealed to the frame. When it's turned on, the house air pressure drops lower than the air pressure outside, which starts drawing outdoor air in through leaks. The auditor can use a thermal imaging camera and a pressure gauge between rooms to determine where the major leaks are occurring. In very leaky homes, you can often feel the air entering.

Local building codes will require a certain level of insulation. When your builder says, "Our houses meet the code," they are basically bragging they got a D on their test. They passed, but just by doing the absolute minimum. In some cases, you'll want to install twice as much R-value as the code says. Everyone will tell you that it's too much and doesn't pay back. They are wrong. But you have to do more than just install additional insulation.

Orient the house correctly. Insulate it and seal it. Put the right windows in the right place with the right protection. Then you will be well on your way to creating a passive solar house.

Do all these things well and you will have a dumb house that shows you are smart. None of them require any care or maintenance—they just sit and work for the life of the structure. You might spend a little more money on insulation, but you will recoup much of that cost in other ways. There is now even an international building standard for this type of house, which is called Passive House (*Passivhaus* in German).

There is also a component called thermal mass, but its effectiveness varies by climate. It is most effective in dry-air climates with large swings between the daytime and nighttime temperature. The simplest explanation is that mass such as concrete, stone, or bricks inside the insulated envelope helps moderate temperature swings. In dry climates with large outdoor temperature differences between day and night, thermal mass can be an important strategy. The right amount of mass can store heat in the warm day and release it in the cool night, smoothing out temperature swings inside.

Those who say too much insulation won't pay back are wrong because they think too narrowly and don't connect the pieces. A house is a system of many different parts and subsystems. Only when you look at the whole system can you understand which pieces have the biggest impact. This is sometimes called integrative or whole-system design. It's the exact opposite of our current linear design process, where specialist after specialist hands off the plans with little overall coordination or whole-system thinking.

House Construction System

Most houses are still constructed using lumber pieced together on site. This practice evolved from large multi-home subdivision construction, where many homes were being built at the same time. However, this method produces a lot of waste and inconsistency. It's the equivalent of going to the auto parts store, buying all the parts, and assembling your car in the driveway. A car is built in a factory where all elements can be controlled and waste minimized. It's a more efficient system and keeps the cost of the car down and the quality up. Fortunately, there are some companies that are building high-quality prefabricated homes, but they are still far outnumbered by the old on-site "stick-built" method.

With either prefab or on-site construction, the most common construction is the stud wall system, where a wooden 2×4 or 2×6 is spaced every 16" or 24" and the wall sections are framed out of these sticks. If you remember "The Three Little Pigs," the house of sticks wasn't the worst construction, but it wasn't the best, either. That story needs to be updated, because bricks are usually just a surface covering and don't reflect the actual structure of the home. Furthermore, a straw-bale home can be quite solid and well insulated.

One problem with stick-built construction is thermal bridging. To minimize the bridging, external insulation board can be used, but it's still not ideal. There are a few engineered frame systems, often called Advanced Framing, that seem to address most of the issues. Some use thicker studs and an external insulation, while others use offset studs to reduce bridging. Still others use 2×6 lumber spaced on 24" centers instead of 16" centers, which reduces thermal bridging by reducing the number of studs. Exterior insulation board reduces it further.

When we were planning our home, I analyzed many types of building systems. The best value (minimum cost for maximum insulation and quality and minimum infiltration) was a structural insulated panel (SIP) system. SIPs are high-performance building panels that can be used for floors, walls, and roofs for residential and light commercial buildings. They are manufactured by sandwiching a core of rigid foam insulation between two structural facings, such as oriented strand board (OSB). Other skin materials can be used for specific purposes.

These SIPs have many advantages: They are built in a controlled environment and customized at the factory. The window and door openings are all precut and trimmed out very accurately. The outlet and switch slots are precut with pull strings for the electrician to easily install wiring without drilling many holes through studs. The insulation is consistent (no thermal bridging) and airtight (no infiltration).

The panels for our house were all numbered, stacked on a flatbed truck, and delivered to the job site. Three workers and a crane quickly assembled the house in a few days. My manufacturer produced panels up to 24' long and 8' high, so it took just a few panels to form the exterior walls. The roof panels were also SIPs, and all lifted in place very quickly. The manufacturer even built the interior stud walls at the factory and stacked them on the truck. Once on site, the workers just stood them up and attached them to the floor.

We chose locally built SIPs made with polystyrene foam under OSB skins. We used six-inch-thick wall panels (R-22) and eight-inch-thick roof panels (R-32). If I were building again, I would choose even higher insulation values by using thicker panels or panels with polyurethane insulation in the sandwich. (Polyurethane has a higher R-value per inch of thickness.)

Before I chose SIPs, the other systems I reviewed were insulated concrete forms (ICF), geodesic domes, concrete spray-on domes, underground, and standard stick-built 2×6 with extra insulation. Some companies are now prefabricating even more of the home structure offsite and quickly assembling the pieces at the job site. There weren't many prefab homes around in the mid-1990s—SIP was as close as I was able to get. There might have been suppliers, but I wasn't aware of them.

The answer to "which system is best?" will be different for different climates and locations. Some areas will benefit more from superinsulation, while others will benefit more from thermal mass. Whatever system you choose, it needs to have very low air leakage. This can be verified using a blower-door test. The important process is to review the available systems, list the pros and cons of each, and compare the cost to the performance. Don't look for lowest cost—look for highest value. And remember, for the best solution you'll need to iterate. Optimizing the wall system (and insulation value) has to be done in conjunction with window and roof selection, and also depends on the efficiency of the layout and the orientation of the home. You have to think beyond just the insulation value. If you "over insulate" the house, use extremely efficient windows, insulate the slab, and take the many other steps people will tell you are overkill, then what happens to the cooling and heating systems? Is it possible you can eliminate them? Or perhaps you've reduced the load so much it opens other paths. Before you consider this system optimized and declare victory, you have to look all the way through the project to make sure you've solved for the whole system, not just a subsystem.

Windows

In the earlier discussion of radiant heat, I used the campfire example. If you took a simple pane of window glass out to a campfire and put it in front of your face, you would still feel most of the radiant heat coming through. However, if you held a pane of low-e glass between yourself and the fire, it would dramatically reduce the heat reaching your face.

Low-e glass will block long-wave (infrared) radiation. So how does low-e glass in your windows help you in your home? On a warm summer day, all the things outside of your house are absorbing solar energy and heating up. They begin to emit long-wave (infrared) radiation. That radiation passes through a typical window pane and strikes you, which makes you feel warmer. Your response is to go turn the air conditioner setting to a colder temperature to compensate for that warm feeling. If you have low-e windows, they will block that radiation and allow you to feel more comfortable at a higher temperature. This allows you to use your air-conditioner less for the same comfort level while saving energy and money.

A simple single-pane window with an aluminum frame has an R-value of about one. That's not good. Even a poorly constructed and minimally insulated wall will be at least seven times better at reducing the transmission of heat. But windows provide other value with natural light, views, and ventilation. The key is to put in the right windows in the right locations with the right shading.

Fortunately, double-pane windows have been available for many decades. There are also triple, quadruple, and even higher-performing assemblies available. Better frame materials are available, as well as insulated spacers that go between the panes of glass. Some manufacturers use a film as one of the internal panes. The film can also be a low-e material.

Choosing the window frame is another decision. Aluminum is low cost and low maintenance, but very conductive. Some aluminum frames have a thermal break, which helps some. Many people like the look of wood, but it is only a modest insulator, and it has high maintenance requirements over time. Vinyl is inexpensive and better insulating than aluminum. It's low maintenance, though the quality can vary across manufacturers. When done well, it's a good choice. Fiberglass is probably the best choice, though it's more expensive than vinyl. It has good insulation, is very low maintenance, and is very stable.

There are a couple of side benefits to quality windows—they will eliminate condensation on the inside glass or frame in the winter, and they will reduce noise transmitted from outside the house. They will also reduce noise transmitted from inside the house, if that's a problem your household presents to your neighborhood.

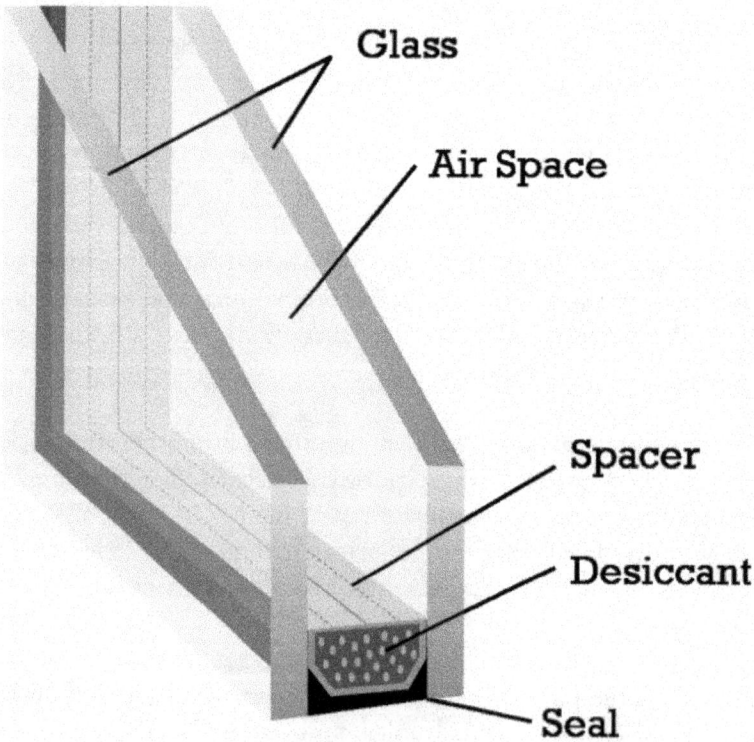

Image source: Glass Doctor

Figure 21. Double-pane window cross-section

These are the key metrics to consider in window selection:

- **Overall U-value:** This indicates the conductivity of the window assembly. (Make sure this is for the assembly, not just the center of glass.) Lower is better. The inverse of this number is the R-value.

- **Solar Heat Gain Coefficient (SHGC):** This is a number between zero and one that tells you how much of the solar energy hitting the window will transmit to the interior. If you live in a hot climate, you'll want a very low number. If you live in a cold climate, balance this number to allow some solar transmission in the winter, especially for equator-facing windows.

- **Visible Light Transmission (VLT or VT):** This is the amount of daylight that passes through a window, expressed as a number between zero and one. In general, you'll want a high number for more daylight, but it has to be balanced with the SHGC number to manage incoming heat.

- **Air Leakage:** This shows how tightly constructed the window assembly is. It is usually a fractional number that indicates how many cubic square feet of air would leak through the assembly per square foot of the assembly (cfm/sf). A lower number is better.

Most windows carry a standardized label to help you find this information. The National Fenestration Rating Council (NFRC) is an international coalition that administers testing, certification, and labeling of windows, skylights, and doors. The NFRC label will show the four numbers above to help you compare and optimize the glazing.

There are many online tools available to help with window selection. One is the Efficient Windows Collaborative (http://www.efficientwindows.org/).

Remember, placement and overhangs are important. You could choose slightly different properties for windows on the various faces of a home. For example, using a better (lower) SHGC on east and west windows can cut down on unwanted heat gain. Or you could use a window on the pole-facing side with a better (higher) VLT and a lower SHGC, as these windows won't get as much direct solar exposure.

As for quantity, there are a few guiding rules that will get you started. Remember, a good energy model should be used to help fine-tune your window area and location. You need to balance views, daylight, solar gain in winter, and conduction loss all year. For a passive solar house, one general guideline is to divide the total window surface area by the house floor area. The result should be in the 10%–15% range. Our house is 16%, so we're close. Boosting this number a bit provides better daylighting with a small energy penalty.

The next consideration is the location of the windows. Most should be on the equator side. I've seen a suggestion that at least 60% of the total window area should be on the equator side. Our house has 61% of the windows on that side.

Generally, the surface area of windows on your equator side divided by your wall surface area should equal your latitude. If you live at latitude 30°, then 30% of the equator-side wall should be glass. If you are at 50° latitude, then 50% should be. This rule of thumb comes from the fact that the farther toward the pole you move, the more glass you'll need to absorb the low-angle winter sun. Our house is at 33° latitude, and 31% of our south wall is glass. This guideline probably works up to a point, but remember that you can also control solar gain with proper overhang sizing.

These guides are great places to start, but a good energy model can help you fine-tune parameters and optimize the entire design for your specific site.

The windows we chose were CertainTeed New Castle Vinyl. They are double-pane, argon-filled, and have a low-e coating. We chose vinyl frames because they were low maintenance and had lower thermal conduction than most other materials. I'm happy to report that these windows were made well—we haven't had a single fogged-up pane in over 22 years, which means the air seals have not failed on a single window.

Roof

The roof faces the sun for more hours of the day than any other part of your home, and it faces the highest intensity sun. If you live in a warm climate, it's the best place to begin heat rejection. Even in mild climates, avoiding unwanted heat gain during warmer weather will more than offset a little reduction in beneficial heat gain during the winter. Many people refer to roofs that reflect heat away as "cool roofs."

Reflectivity indicates the ability of the roof to reflect the direct rays from the sun. A cool roof will reflect at least 65% of the energy away, which earns a 0.65 reflectivity rating. Look for this rating or better.

The other number to look for is **emissivity**. Emissivity is the ability of a roof to re-radiate any energy absorbed back to the sky. This energy is in the form of that long-wave infrared heat discussed previously. It is expressed as a decimal between 0 and 1, and higher is better. A higher number means the roof will more easily radiate away any absorbed energy.

In roof specifications, you'll also see a **Solar Reflective Index (SRI)** number. The SRI considers both reflectivity and emissivity to score the overall energy performance of a roof material. Look for the initial and three-year aged data to see how well the product holds up over time, and remember, higher numbers are better.

The SRI is a good measure of roof reflectivity, indicating the constructed surface's ability to stay cool in the sun by reflecting solar radiation and emitting thermal radiation. A standard black surface with initial solar reflectance of 0.05 and initial thermal emittance of 0.90 will have an initial SRI of 0. A standard white surface (initial solar reflectance of 0.80, initial thermal emittance of 0.90) has an initial SRI of 100. Simply think of it as a 0 to 100 scale, with 100 being best.

You can review the characteristics of various roof materials at the following sites:

- Cool Roof Ratings Council: coolroofs.org
- Energy Star:
  http://www.energystar.gov/products/building_products/roof_products

Note that U.S. Energy Star requirements are less stringent than some other codes and standards; nevertheless, picking an Energy Star choice is still better than choosing for price or color. At least get the numbers and evaluate your roof choices with energy efficiency in mind so you can make an educated decision.

There is another alternative to a cool roof, which is a green roof. This is a flat roof covered with soil and plants. Soil by itself is not a great insulator, so insulation is installed below the waterproof membrane. The mass of the soil helps moderate the temperature the roof material is exposed to and shields it from the elements, giving it a very long life. Green roofs slow rain runoff, which provides some downstream flood risk reduction.

There are numerous roof choices, and your best choice depends on several factors, such as your climate and roof slope. If you have a flat or low-slope roof you can consider installing a white membrane roof, such as PVC and TPO membranes or EPDM rubber.

For the Westbrook House, we chose a standing-seam metal roof for a few reasons. One was durability—it will probably last 50+ years or more. Second, it's recyclable. We won't be filling up the landfill with asphalt shingle replacements every decade or so, as we would have with a typical roof. Third, it is fairly reflective. We chose a bare Galvalume material. Choosing a light-colored, coated metal roof would reflect even more heat away, but I worried the coating might be a weak point. (Data over time, however, seems to indicate the coatings are quite robust.) My bare Galvalume roof has good reflectivity but poor emissivity. It's still much better than the typical dark asphalt shingle that builders in our area tend to use.

Metal roofs' SRI scores depend on their color. A medium to dark asphalt shingle will have an SRI between 4 and 9. My bare Galvalume roof has an SRI of 43. A similar metal roof with a white coating would have an SRI over 70.

In addition to its energy and resource efficiency benefits, the metal roof is also very fire-resistant and is a better surface for rainwater collection, as asphalt roofs shed small particles and leach chemicals.

My Galvalume standing-seam metal roof was twice the cost of an asphalt shingle roof—but remember, I only had to pay that once, so in the long run I'll be way ahead financially. The roof offers some payback with energy savings, but the biggest savings kicked in after Texas passed a law mandating discounts for hail-resistant roofing. In Texas, we frequently have large hailstorms, and they cause billions of dollars in roof damage. The state therefore mandated insurance companies provide a price break on home insurance based on the hail resistance rating of the roof material. Our roof was the top-rated, a 22-gauge metal that had a Class Four rating (the best of four classes). I've enjoyed a 23% discount on my home insurance for twenty years and counting, which has more than paid the extra cost for the better roof, and is well on the way to paying for the roof entirely. And that's a roof that will probably outlive me. I chose it for energy efficiency, and there is a slow payback there, but the real savings comes from its durability and insurance discount.

Remember the integrative design lesson: I designed the house as a compact two-story house to minimize the amount of roof and slab area. I made the roof smaller to help with energy efficiency. This meant I needed less roofing material, so it was easier to afford a higher quality roof material. It's all connected.

Underground Movement

I considered an underground house, but thought SIPs were the best option for us. However, our site sloped slightly from west to east, so we decided to berm the side of our garage into the hill. The west wall of our garage is earth-bermed up to about 42" high, providing a large thermal advantage. The soil temperature in our area averages about 69°F. Just a few feet down, the temperature stays constant year-round, and our garage is coupled to that stable temperature. We insulated the garage and purchased an insulated garage door. The garage only cools down to the 50s in the winter, even when it's below freezing outside. It only climbs to the 80s in the summer despite 100°F outside temperatures.

The garage is integrated into the house structure rather than being a separate building, which helps the energy performance of both. A portion of our conditioned space abuts the garage, which stays at a much more moderate temperature than the outdoors. We still used SIPs between the conditioned space and the garage, but those SIP panels have much lighter thermal challenge.

House Systems

If you build a correctly-oriented, well-insulated, and airtight shell, then you do things very differently inside as well.

First, you can either eliminate your air conditioner and/or heater, or you can shrink them down dramatically in size. You don't need to set up zoning because the temperature stays uniform all through a very well-insulated house. The house just got a little dumber (little or no zone control), but simpler and less expensive.

Second, if you do need air conditioning and/or heating in this efficient structure you will be purchasing a much smaller unit, which will save both initial and operating costs. You can use some of those savings to purchase a more efficient unit, which will generate further operational savings.

Third, because the house is so airtight you'll need to install an energy recovery ventilator (ERV). This unit exhausts air from the bathrooms and kitchen through a heat exchanger, which can recover a good portion of the outgoing energy. The ERV then brings a stream of fresh, filtered air into the unit and tempers that air with the recovered energy. You get a nice supply of filtered, fresh air with minimal energy penalty. And your house will have much less dust and fewer pests.

Energy Recovery Ventilator (ERV)

There are two main types of ventilators available. A Heat Recovery Ventilator (HRV) only recovers a portion of the air temperature energy. It doesn't exchange any moisture. The ERV also recovers some of the air's moisture content.

To understand the difference, assume it's a cold and dry winter day. An ERV uses a desiccant wheel that rotates slowly between the incoming fresh air and the outgoing exhaust air stream. The desiccant material absorbs moisture and transfers it to the drier air stream along with the heat. In the winter, it moves heat and moisture to the incoming cold, dry air stream. An HRV would warm the incoming air, but it wouldn't add any moisture, so the air in your house might be too dry.

In the summer, the ERV removes heat and moisture from the incoming fresh air stream. An HRV would cool the incoming air stream, but it would not reduce the moisture content. Our ERV is about 75% thermally efficient, even after more than twenty years of operation. Figure 22 shows the summer and winter operation modes.

Energy Recovery Ventilator (ERV)

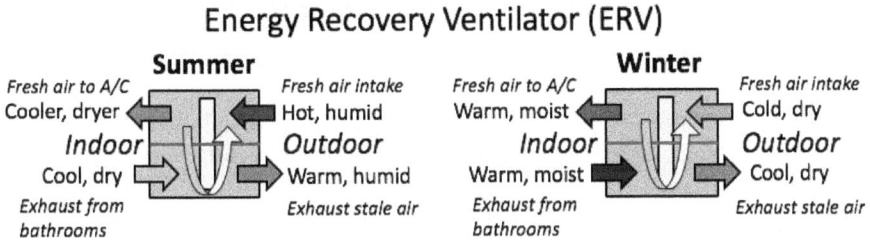

Summer

Fresh air to A/C
Cooler, dryer

Indoor
Cool, dry

Exhaust from
bathrooms

Fresh air intake
Hot, humid

Outdoor
Warm, humid

Exhaust stale air

Winter

Fresh air to A/C
Warm, moist

Indoor
Warm, moist

Exhaust from
bathrooms

Fresh air intake
Cold, dry

Outdoor
Cool, dry

Exhaust stale air

Figure 22. Energy recovery ventilator (ERV)

The ERV replaces multiple ventilation fans in various rooms. It's a central system with ducts run to each room that requires ventilation. This reduces the quantity of small, inefficient bathroom fans and the holes in your roof or wall needed to exhaust the air.

If you are longing for some smart house appliances, the ERV would be a decent place to start. With a little monitoring and control, it's easy to optimize this appliance for the best balance of comfort and efficiency.

Heating and Air Conditioning

Heating, Ventilating, and Air Conditioning (HVAC) is the system that provides fresh air and temperature control in our homes. If you live in a cool climate that predominantly requires heating, you can eliminate or significantly reduce your heating needs with a well-insulated and airtight building combined with passive solar techniques. A cold-climate passive solar house is the type that can benefit the most from thermal mass. A large amount of mass in the conditioned space can help even out temperature swings between day and night. The mass absorbs extra solar heat during the day and releases it into the house slowly overnight. A concrete foundation is a good mass, provided you've insulated the perimeter and even under the slab in the coldest climates. (Concrete is a relatively good thermal conductor and will readily lose heat to the outdoors—especially along the exposed strip of slab above the soil.) Other indoor thermal mass can come from decorative brick or stone features or water stored in tanks.

If you need supplemental heat, there are various options. One approach is radiant floor heat, most often using a hydronic system in which tubing is placed in the building slab with warm water circulated through it. As the floor warms, the heat rises into the house. It's a nice way to heat, because if your feet are warm you'll feel much more comfortable. The hot water can come from a variety of sources. Solar is best, but you can also use gas and/or electric heat as the primary source or as a supplement to solar. If you only need space heating and not any cooling, then radiant floor heating is a good system. There are also radiant wall panels available.

High-efficiency natural gas or propane heaters can deliver heat fairly efficiently for either radiant heating or a forced-air distribution system. In a forced-air system the heat is distributed through the air via ductwork.

For climates where cooling is needed, there are several possible approaches. A typical air conditioning unit uses a compression cycle to generate cool air and dehumidify the air. A heat pump is an air conditioner that can reverse the cycle to provide heat. If you need both heating and cooling, this is an economical approach, as you have one unit that handles both tasks fairly efficiently.

Unfortunately, most builders and installers just install units that meet the minimum requirements. They think only of first cost and not of lifetime operating costs. Our home's cooling system, which was installed in 1996 when the code required a minimum SEER of twelve, operates at almost twice that efficiency. The savings from 22 years of operating that unit have far exceeded any additional purchase cost.

Typical heat pumps either remove heat to, or extract heat from, the outside air. When temperatures get close to freezing, these units become inefficient and must resort to a backup heating system, typically electric resistance heating—which is about the *least* efficient way to heat. A compression cycle is about three to four times more efficient than electric resistance heating. There is an even more efficient heat pump available: a geothermal or ground-source heat pump (GSHP). Instead of air, a GSHP uses the stable temperature of the soil to provide heat or dissipate it. Just a few feet down, the earth's temperature is very stable year-round, generally around the average annual air temperature for your location. By placing tubing in the ground—either horizontally or vertically—you can use a glycol/water mixture to turn the earth into a giant heat exchanger.

To understand how this works, look at the compression cooling cycle for a typical air-source heat pump. In cooling mode, the compressor pressurizes a working fluid (refrigerant). This compression raises the refrigerant's temperature to more than 140°F. Then it goes outside to the box with the fan and coils (condenser). The refrigerant flows through the coils while the fan blows air across them to remove heat. Even on a 100°F day, the 140°F working fluid will give up some heat. Next, the refrigerant goes through an expansion valve. Expanding, it cools it down to around 45°F. This cool refrigerant flows through the coil in your house (evaporator), where a fan blows across the coil to cool and dehumidify the air. This is the cool air delivered through your duct and vents. In winter, the cycle reverses. The compressed refrigerant releases heat into your home and the expanded refrigerant goes outside to absorb more heat.

A GSHP works the same way, except the outdoor (condenser) unit is replaced by a small heat exchanger that attaches to the loop of fluid in the ground pipes.

Distributed refrigerant systems are another alternative. These systems don't use ductwork, but instead move the refrigerant from room to room with small tubing. Each room that needs it has a small fan coil unit mounted on the wall. These systems begin to look attractive if you have a very well-insulated house with little variation in cooling or heating needs between various rooms. Just a couple of fan coil units can manage the entire house. They aren't as efficient as a ground-source heat pump since they still use an outdoor air-cooled unit, but they are often variable speed and can be quite efficient. There are also financial and space savings from not having to distribute ductwork across the house.

Internal Loads

We've already covered several ways to reduce the external heating and cooling loads in your house. Now let's look at the internal loads. Almost everything that uses electricity converts a large portion of that electricity to heat. This heat adds to the cooling load of your home. If you live in a warm climate, that's just additional heat the air conditioner needs to remove. If you live in a cold climate, you might think this "waste" heat is good. However, there are much more efficient ways to produce heat. Always choose the most efficient lighting and appliances.

Consider an old-fashioned incandescent light bulb that uses 60W of energy to produce 800 lumens (lum) of light. The efficiency can be measured in lumens per watt (lum/W): 800 lumens/60W = 18.3 lum/W, which is not very good. Most of that electrical energy is being converted to heat. You don't have a light bulb; you have a small 60W electric resistance heater producing 204.7 Btu/hr (60W x 3.412 Btu/W). That heat must then be removed by your air conditioner. If the air conditioner has a 14 SEER rating, it will cool at a rate of 14 Btu/W-hr. Therefore, to cool that load requires 14.6 W.

A good rule of thumb for an electrical appliance is to round up the watt rating by 20–25% to account for the cooling energy required. A 60W incandescent bulb therefore *really* uses 75W (60 to produce light and 15 to remove the waste heat).

If you are in a cold climate you might think waste heat is okay, but other heating systems can produce heat far more efficiently. If you are in a climate where you are trying to cool off most of the year, then it's definitely a bad idea to install so many unintentional space heaters in your home.

Water Heating

Water heating is often a significant portion of home energy consumption. Electric water heaters use a resistance coil to convert electricity to heat. Gas water heaters combust fuel to produce heat, which is transferred to the water. In general, a gas heater is more energy-efficient than electric, but there are other efficient approaches available.

Tankless water heaters get a lot of press, but the only energy they save is from eliminating standby losses from hot water sitting in a large tank waiting for you to use it. If you have a well-insulated tank, these standby losses are minimal. There is a much better way to heat water—solar.

Since 1985, I've been heating water with solar energy. It's not quite free, as I have to power a couple of very small pumps to circulate the water that collects the heat, but it's a fractional cost compared to heating water with electricity or gas. Solar systems like mine can also incorporate electric or gas heaters for backup.

There are several types of solar water-heating systems, and the best choice for you depends on your climate. If you live where it never freezes, then a simple batch heater or a thermosiphon system might be the best choice. There are no pumps or controls, so these systems are very simple. The batch heater is a tank that sits on the roof under glass. The glass helps trap incoming heat so it can be absorbed by the water in the tank. Such heaters often use a reflective back surface to aim the sun's rays at the tank. If you live in a nonfreezing climate, your incoming water is probably fairly warm, so a batch heater will easily boost your water temperature to the needed setting. A thermosiphon system uses flat-plate panels to heat the water, placed at a level slightly below the tank, which eliminates the need for a pump. The cooler, denser water in the tank "falls" toward the collectors, where it is heated and rises back toward the top of the tank. It's nature's pump.

For climates where freezing is possible, there are two major types of freeze-protection systems: drain-back and closed-loop, with a few variations of each type. Both systems use a heat exchanger to move heat from the working fluid (that travels to the solar collector) to the household water. Both systems use a flat-plate collector or evacuated tube collector to capture the sun's energy. Flat-plate collectors are simpler and adequate for most climates. The evacuated tube collectors perform better in colder, cloudier climates. However, they introduce another potential point of failure with multiple evacuated glass tubes. Both systems have a differential thermostat, which uses a pair of sensors to check the temperature at the collector and the temperature at the bottom of the storage tank. When the temperature at the collectors exceeds the tank temperature by a set amount, the pumps turn on. When the temperature is equalized, the pumps turn off. Both of these systems use a heat exchanger to transfer the energy and isolate the two water loops from each other.

With this basic pump-and-thermostat design, there are two primary means of keeping water from freezing in the rooftop panels. One approach is a drain-back system, which uses one pump to lift the working fluid to the collector. When that pump is off, the fluid drains back to a reservoir tank in the conditioned space, so there is no risk of freezing. Because the pump has to overcome gravity to move the fluid up, this design usually requires a slightly higher pump energy. In addition, there is often a second, smaller pump to move water from the storage tank through the heat exchanger.

The other freeze-protection method is a closed-loop system, which runs a pressurized loop of fluid up to the collectors. The fluid is usually a mix of distilled water and propylene glycol. Because the loop is closed, the pump doesn't have to overcome gravity, just the pressure loss in the piping. As in the drain-back system, a second pump moves water from the storage tank through the heat exchanger.

Recent developments in heat-pump water heaters have opened a new type of solar water heating. A heat-pump water heater is about three times more efficient than an electric-resistance water heater. If the space on the roof designated for flat-plate water heaters were instead used for solar electric panels, then the sun could heat water via the electric heat pump. In a warm climate, this heat pump will "reject" cool air to your conditioned space as well. When I worked with the University of Illinois Solar Decathlon team in 2009, they were the only school to utilize the heat-pump water heater. And they were the only school that scored a perfect score in the water heating tests. By using the roof space for additional solar electric panels, they gained energy flexibility. If they didn't need hot water, then the electricity could be used for anything in the house. With a dedicated solar thermal system, there is usually no alternative use for any excess heat produced by the system during the hottest portion of the year.

In 1996, we chose a closed-loop solar water-heating system for our own house. I bought some used Lennox flat-plate panels for $100 each. They were manufactured in 1978 and were still working fine in 2018, the time of this writing. For a storage tank, I chose an all-plastic electric water heater made by Marathon. At some point after my purchase, Marathon was acquired by Rheem, but they still call them Marathon units. The all-plastic tank won't corrode like other water heater materials. Marathon provided a full lifetime warranty, and when, after 19 years, mine developed a leak around one of the connection joints at the top of the unit, Rheem replaced it for free. This tank has a full R-25 insulation jacket all around it, so it retains heat much longer than traditional units. I added a tee to the drain valve at the bottom and to the relief valve port at the top, then connected a loop of piping through one side of a heat exchanger. This loop has a small pump to circulate water through the exchanger. On the other side of the heat exchanger, I ran a loop of piping up to the roof to flow through the solar flat-plate panels. The roof loop also has a small pump, which is filled with a mixture of propylene glycol and water for freeze protection.

My roof panels are tilted up at an angle of 45 degrees. This angle is my latitude plus twelve degrees. A good design rule for solar water-heating panels is to angle them at your latitude plus fifteen degrees to optimize for the low winter sun. I rounded down to twelve degrees so the result was a 45 degree angle, which made it easier to convey to the welder who built the rack for the panels.

The pumps are controlled by a differential temperature controller. This unit has two temperature sensors. One mounts to the outlet pipe (drain valve pipe) at the bottom of the tank, where water is the coldest. The other sensor mounts at the outlet of the solar panel. It's set so when the panel temperature is 8°F warmer than the bottom of the tank, the pumps turn on and begin circulating the fluids. The hot fluid from the roof passes through the counterflow heat exchanger and gives up the heat to the water loop that comes from the bottom of the tank and flows back into the top. When the sensors reach equal temperatures, the controller turns off.

Lighting

For a home, electric lighting is a large energy load. Designing the structure to maximize natural daylight can reduce energy needs. Remember, in most situations the goal is to get the light without the direct sun rays that carry heat. This is best done with polar-facing windows (north in the northern hemisphere) or equator-facing windows with properly sized overhangs. East and west-facing windows make it very hard to control unwanted heat gain, and they provide harsh, intense light early and late in the day.

When you install lighting, make it efficient and controlled. Controls can consist of anything from simple light switches to motion-sensor switches to timers to full computer control. If you can develop the good habit of only turning on lights when you need them, then a simple manual switch might be all you need. (All lighting is efficient when it's off.)

Lighting comes in a wide range of efficiency. For example, let's compare an incandescent bulb, a compact fluorescent bulb (CF), and an LED bulb. Remember wattage is not a measure of light output—lumens are how you measure the level of light. Wattage is the power it takes to produce that light. Lighting efficiency is measured in lum/W. Many LED bulbs can produce more than 100 lum/W. The traditional 60W incandescent used 60W to produce 800 lumens (13 lum/W), where a modern LED only uses about 8W to provide the same illumination (100 lum/W).

This is probably a good place to point out the evils of recessed or "can" lighting. Because they usually penetrate from a living space into an attic, recessed fixtures create multiple energy penalties. The first one is by creating holes in the ceiling/roof insulation. That space needs to be well insulated and airtight, but recessed lighting protrudes into the insulation and lowers its effectiveness. Some fixtures need to have the insulation cleared around them so they aren't a fire hazard. In addition, recessed fixtures often leak air. Remember when I talked about a negative attic pressure sucking the conditioned air out of the house? A recessed light is an easy airflow path to negative pressure. If you want downlight spots, then use a track light that doesn't penetrate the insulation barrier.

For our house, we chose light fixtures that mounted to the ceiling fans we have in most rooms, then installed a couple of track light channels on the bottom of support beams where we wanted some spot lighting.

Appliances

For all appliances, look at their Energy Star rating and reliability data. You don't necessarily need to spend more to get quality and efficiency. Often the most expensive appliances have an excess of bells and whistles, which end up making them less reliable—i.e., more things to break. Think of the old quote, "Make things as simple as possible, but not simpler." Elegant simplicity is good.

I rely on Energy Star data, which can be found online, for energy and water use information. I utilize *Consumer Reports* for reliability data. Just sorting a large list of available appliances by those two criteria can quickly narrow it down to a handful of choices for final consideration. Once you get down to the top few, you can then comparison shop, test them, and search for the best price on the one you prefer.

If you buy an efficient appliance with a good history of reliability and don't go crazy on fancy features, then you'll get many years of service and minimize your energy and water consumption. We chose well on appliances.

Our refrigerator was a very efficient 1996 model and lasted about fourteen years. The replacement was significantly more efficient due to better design. The dishwasher lasted nineteen years, and the new model improved slightly on efficiency. Since water heating is a large part of the dishwasher energy use, and our water is solar heated, any model would be very efficient. We installed an early model of the horizontal axis washing machine. It worked well on the clothes, but had some balancing issues in the spin cycle, which caused leaking. Fortunately, it was located in a utility room with a floor drain, so the leaking was not a big issue. We eventually replaced that with a Bosch horizontal axis unit that does a great job of cleaning with minimal water use and no maintenance issues. We use an electric dryer, which is a big energy user, but the horizontal axis washing machine does a better job of spinning much of the water out, so the drying time is reduced.

If I built another house, I would strongly consider installing two dishwashers and fewer storage cabinets. Using a dishwasher to wash dishes is more efficient than doing them by hand. However, we spend a lot of time unloading dishes that go back in the drawers and cabinets only to use them and put them back in the dishwasher. What about having a pair of dishwashers and alternating between them? You would just pull your dishes, glasses, and silverware from the clean one (dishwasher A), then load up the other one when they are dirty (dishwasher B). Once enough dirty dishes have transferred over, run unit B. Then pull clean dishes from unit B as needed and drop the dirty ones back in A. That's more efficient than unloading the dishwasher and putting your most commonly used dishes and silverware back into cabinets and drawers. A side benefit is you have a redundant dishwasher in case one breaks down. Finally, dishwashers are at an accessible height, so as I age it becomes easier to access the dishes.

Refrigerator

This single appliance will probably use more energy than any other appliance in the house. An electric dryer uses more power, but runs for only a few hours each week, and it could be replaced with a clothesline if desired. The refrigerator is always operating. Again, use the energy and reliability data to narrow your choices. There is a wide range of efficiency available, so don't just select your refrigerator based on color or features alone.

And please don't add an extra refrigerator and/or freezer, and especially don't put one out in a hot garage. Placing an appliance that is trying to cool in what is often the hottest area of the house further lowers the efficiency. Being more diligent about managing the space in your one refrigerator/freezer is the most efficient choice. Buy one high-quality appliance and manage the use.

Plug Loads

The same process used for selecting a refrigerator/freezer should be used for all other appliances in the house. Use the energy and reliability ratings to narrow the list down. The TV can be a large energy user, and TVs have really grown in size. Plasma TVs were notorious energy hogs, but most have moved to LCD and LED, which can be much more efficient.

Also, many appliances draw large amounts of energy when they are OFF. It's commonly called vampire power because it's sucking electrons at night while you aren't using it. There are a few ways to combat this "vampire" power use. First, look for products that have no, or low power use when off. Next, consider putting some appliances on a switched power outlet so you can fully turn them off. We have our microwave on a switch—I don't need to see the clock for the 23.9 hours per day we aren't cooking something in the microwave.

There are some "smart" outlets where one item can control the others. If you have several items that you use with the TV, such as a DVD player and an amplifier for speakers, you can plug the TV into the master outlet and the other appliances into the controlled outlets. When the TV turns off, a sensor in the plug strip turns off the controlled outlets and stops the vampire power draw by other appliances. Obviously, you can't use these with a TV recording device, but there are many appliances that can be turned off completely when they aren't in use.

Energy Generation

You could run your house on a gasoline or propane generator if you wanted. It would probably be very expensive electricity, but you could do it. You can produce your own electricity from several sources. For a typical residence, the most environmentally friendly system is solar photovoltaic (PV). It's also becoming the most cost-effective. There are also residential scale wind turbines available.

There are several ways to hook up a solar PV system. The completely off-grid version requires energy storage—most often batteries. The PV panels produce energy in direct current (DC) and can charge the batteries. The battery energy can be used in the house. In a few cases, people will just use DC appliances and use the energy directly. Most people use an inverter to convert to alternating current (AC) so they can use typical appliances.

Most people who have a fairly reliable electric grid will install a grid-connected system. There are two different methods: a central inverter (also known as a string inverter) and distributed inverters (known as microinverters). The central inverter method connects all the panels in a DC string and brings that DC power to the inverter, where it is converted to AC electricity. The downside is the string of panels will only perform at the level of the lowest performing panel. If one panel has a defect or excessive shade, then the whole string of panels will not perform up to their potential. There are some DC optimizers that can be placed at each panel to help overcome this weakness. Also, the wiring is in DC, which is less well understood by electricians and code officials because it's not as common. The advantage of a DC system is it can directly feed a battery bank for storage.

The distributed inverter method uses a small inverter at each panel that converts to AC—hence the term microinverter. These connect to an AC trunk cable and feed a double pole breaker. It's essentially like hooking up an electric dryer in reverse. Electricians and code officials will naturally feel more comfortable with this type of system. The microinverters can report their individual production, which helps in system monitoring and troubleshooting. Each microinverter is optimizing its individual panel, so one bad panel doesn't spoil the whole bunch. If one inverter goes out, then you only lose a small amount of production. When a central inverter goes down, the whole system is offline. The downside of the microinverter method is it makes storage more difficult. The microinverters need to see grid power to synchronize and allow the solar panels to produce electricity.

Inverters (both central and distributed) on a grid-connected system must see the grid power in order to synchronize the power frequency. If the grid goes down, these units disconnect from the grid. The main reason is safety. If a local lineman is working on a power line and you are backfeeding power to the grid, the lineman could get an unexpected shock. Once the power comes back on there is a short time delay until the inverter can reconnect. This is governed by a safety standard: UL1741.

A grid-connected system can also have energy storage, but it becomes a bit more complex. You have to be able to completely disconnect from the grid so you don't backfeed energy when running off the battery system.

The principles discussed for PV also apply for residential wind turbines. In 2006, we installed one of the first Skystream home wind generators in the country (Figure 23). I was a beta tester for the product. We didn't have the ideal site, as we had trees too close to the tower. It was a 2.4kW turbine on a 35-foot tall monopole. Since the power output varies at the cube of the wind speed, my unit was severely hampered. The trees slowed the wind and produced eddy currents that caused the turbine to hunt for the direction and pulse up and down in speed. I was producing about 1/8th the power I would have on a clear site. Like real estate, the three most important things for wind energy is location (good wind zone), location (no obstructions), location (tall tower). We are in a moderate wind zone, I had too many trees nearby, and I could only get the 35-foot tower on my site—they offered me a 50-foot tower, but I didn't have the room to install it. The wind turbine was certainly a local landmark. I called it the kinetic lawn sculpture.

We had been interested in installing solar PV for many years, but our electric provider (Grayson-Collin Electric Cooperative—GCEC) didn't offer any incentives like providers in adjacent utility distribution areas. The only incentive available is the 30% federal tax credit.

By 2012, PV panel prices had fallen so low it began to look like it would be feasible to install a system. Plus, my money in the bank is earning such a small amount of interest, I figured I could get a much better return investing in renewable energy generation. I analyzed my three previous years of electric use to size the system. The electric utility will not credit or pay me for production beyond my monthly consumption, so the economical approach is to zero-out the low use month. My meter is allowed to turn backward and credit me for excess production during the month. Using the PV watts program (https://pvwatts.nrel.gov/), I figured the optimal size PV system would be about 3.3kW = (14) 240W panels.

With no local incentives I had to keep the cost low, so I started reviewing various designs and components. I found PV panels via Craigslist. They are Sharp 240W panels that are "B" grade. That designation means there might be a cosmetic flaw, but there is no problem with the solar panel energy production, but they do have a short warranty. I got these for $0.85/W delivered, and he even came back to pick up the boxes for reuse after I installed the panels—sweet! The only risk with "B" grade is they have only a 90-day warranty. In general, a panel will fail quickly, so the risk is low. For that price I'm basically self-insured. $200 to replace one bad panel would not be an issue since I saved over $2,000 on the panels.

Figure 23. Westbrook family Skystream wind generator

I decided to use micro-inverters because it makes the installation easy and there are no DC issues to worry about. One micro-inverter is installed for each panel, and it converts the DC output to 120V AC. I selected the Enphase M215 model because of their long experience in the market and long warranty. I found those online for $149 each, delivered. The big advantage of microinverters is each panel's output is optimized instead of the entire string of panels being fed to a single inverter. With the string approach, the worst performing panel will limit the system output. Microinverters let each panel perform at a maximum level.

The next big material cost item is mounting. I have a standing-seam metal roof, which allows me to use one of the non-penetrating seam clamp devices. The original clamp device is the S-5-U. At one point I thought I could use the S-5-U mini with an S-5-PV adapter to simplify the installation at a low cost. However, this would have required a portrait orientation installation, and landscape fit better with my available roof area. I settled on the Unirac Solarmount-I system, which has a one-inch I-beam that can be attached to the roof with the S-5-U clamps.

I did all the material ordering and was able to find good deals on many items via the web and Craigslist. I probably saved at least $0.50/watt by price shopping. I also did a good amount of the labor by mounting all the racks and helping with the final mounting, as well as pulled the permit and did a few other things to minimize the electrician's time on site. This saved me another $0.50/watt.

When I installed the wind turbine we mounted a sub-panel on the side of the house with extra breaker spaces. The solar will connect to a 240V double pole breaker in that panel. The four #10 wires (L1, L2, Neutral, and Ground) run to a junction box on the roof where the Enphase engage cable is connected to the wire. The inverters simply plug into the engage cable.

The panels are grounded to the rails with Unirac ground clips under the edge of the panel. The inverters are grounded with a #8 wire along with the rails. Everything is taken back to the grounding rod below the sub-panel.

Enphase sells a monitoring system that plugs into a home outlet and reads data on each inverter via power line communication. This device connects to the Internet so data can be viewed and tracked. This system was not inexpensive, but knowing how the panels are performing will help me keep the system optimized and at maximum power production. I also mounted a

simple kWh meter next to the breaker box so I can visually see the cumulative production. Link to my data:
https://enlighten.enphaseenergy.com/public/systems/J6RW139890

My total out of pocket cost was $8,844. I did get the 30% federal tax credit, which lowered my total cost to $6,191. My simple payback is about 13 years, but that is a 7% return on my money after taxes. For much of the past decade my savings were earning less than 1% in the bank, and that's before taxes. Solar power is a great investment financially and environmentally.

The solar system performed so well I decided to see if I could sell the wind turbine. It needed to go to a better home where it could spin free in the unobstructed wind. A guy in Oklahoma, where the wind comes sweeping down the plain, bought it—for slightly more than I paid for it. He said he couldn't even see a tree from where he lived. Since I already had power run out to the wind turbine location, I built a small rack and added two more solar panels to bring my system up to 3.7kW total. With other efficiency improvements, we are now producing about 80% of our own electricity on an annual basis—clean, renewable electricity. And we're producing it at about seven cents per kWh instead of the ten-plus cents our utility sells it.

We were already very efficient with our energy use. Combined with our family Prius cars, we have significantly lowered our household fossil fuel footprint. Despite the solid evidence and observations related to the negative impacts of fossil fuel use, our country blindly keeps pursuing the path of drilling, polluting, and ignoring the effects. It's nice to know solutions are available and affordable. We, the people, have the power to change the power industry and save ourselves some money at the same time. Living with less energy and generating electricity with renewable energy allows us to live more comfortably at a lower cost and with a lower burden on the environment and society. What's not to like?

House Design Process and Professionals

I've elaborated on many of the elements that go into good home design. It was an integrative and iterative design process. I can summarize it as follows:

1. Select a good lot with the proper orientation.

2. Set a project budget goal.

3. Select the right builder and architect.

4. List the approximate rooms and sizes desired.

5. Work the layout of those rooms to fit in an optimum shaped house.

    a. Optimize the surface to volume ratio.
    b. Place most windows on the north and south, few on the east and west.
    c. Keep plumbing areas clustered together.
    d. Consider mechanical and electrical system layout and distribution.

6. Perform an energy analysis of the proposed design.

7. Iterate steps two to four a few times until the space is minimized and optimized.

8. Select structural system and components.

9. Run the first rough project cost analysis.

10. Select window locations and sizes—balancing energy, views, daylighting.

11. Run various materials and insulation values through the energy model to optimize the energy performance and cost.

12. If needed, return to step three and make another layout optimization pass.

13. Fine-tune the window sizes, locations, and overhangs.

14. Select plumbing, mechanical, and electrical fixtures with a focus on efficiency.

15. Run a full cost model at this point.

16. Rerun the energy model with updated values.

17. Layout or plan for renewable energy systems.

18. If needed (for cost, energy, or both), return to an earlier step and iterate. Everything is connected, and as you change one thing it impacts several others.

A DFW area couple recently hired me to help them with the process of designing a custom home. They had been on our solar house tour and liked what we did. I'm not going to be their architect or builder, but I'm going to help them find the right ones and assist with the integrative design process. Going through the process with them has been a good reminder for me, so I thought I would document the steps we took with builder and designer selection.

Builders

We started with the builders. I asked a number of contacts for recommendations for builders who understood how to build a quality, efficient home. I ended up with a list of thirteen names. I prepared an email questionnaire to gauge their availability, interest, and experience. Here were the questions:

1. Would you be willing to work on a project in (project location)? If not, thank you for your time and we are open to additional recommendations.

2. Do you have any "green" building experience? What certifications have any of your homes achieved?

3. Do you have experience with any of the following systems:
   a. SIP?
   b. ICF?
   c. Other well-insulated, airtight construction methods?

4. Do you have architects/design people on staff or a preferred list of architects you work with?

5. Have you participated in an integrative design process with the owners, architect, and key suppliers to optimize design and cost?

6. Do you have a $ or $/sf cost range of well-insulated homes you've recently built (and the square footage)?

7. What is your typical contract structure? If cost plus, what is your approximate fee?

8. I've looked at your web site. If there is a particular project you've done that you think is a good representation of this request, please send or direct us to the information.

Only seven of the thirteen responded. The seven that responded seemed qualified enough to make it to the next round. The next step was to set up ~45-minute meetings with each builder individually. This gave the couple a chance to see how their chemistry was, and we could ask builders a few more process-related questions. Some of the additional questions were:

1. Tell us about your process: design, bids, cost/fee, quality?

2. Thoughts on an architect versus an architectural draftsman?

3. On site practices: pre-meeting, quality assurance?

4. Level of job planning during the design: pipe routing, etc.

Only four of the seven decided to attend the interview. One decided he had too much work going already, another said he didn't have time for a meeting, and another never responded.

Note: our process is not starting with a design they are bidding on. The process is to select the right builder and have them intimately involved in the design process. For every hour they spend in design, I think it will save them at least several days on the job site. The goal is to have a buildable design and excellent planning so the construction process runs much smoother. Changes once construction begins are costly and time consuming. And having the construction contractor supply real-time cost feedback during the design means the project will be designed right and fit the budget without the dreaded "value engineering." As Amory Lovins likes to say, "Value engineering is neither."

The four who came all had good qualifications and a variety of experience. All seemed qualified and would do a good job, so it came down to feel at this point. I asked my clients what they thought, and they quickly ranked the four in their preferred order. We agreed we should do further exploration of the top two in parallel to interviewing architects.

Architect/Designer

One of the two builder finalists was a design/build firm, so we decided to review potential architects to see what combo made the most sense. We followed a similar process as our builder search. I asked for recommendations and compiled a list of seven. We sent the following list of questions to the potential designers:

1. Availability/location: Are you available and interested to work on the project in (project location)?

2. Do you have any "green" building/sustainable design/integrative design experience? If so, please elaborate and/or provide accreditations and certifications your homes achieved?

3. I'm a strong advocate of a well-insulated/airtight envelope. Which systems have you used (SIP, ICF, Advanced Framing, etc.)?

4. Have you participated in an integrative design process with the owners, architect, and key suppliers to optimize design and cost?

5. Do you do energy modeling at the start of the project? Which modeling system do you use?

6. What type of design fee structure do you generally use?

7. I've looked at your web site. If there is a particular project you've done that you think is a good representation of this type of project, please send info or direct us to the information.

One of the architects responded he was fairly busy and provided the name of another architect who he thought would be perfect for this project. We ended up with four responses, three of which looked to be very strong, so we set up interviews. Just like the builders, we were already down to the best of their craft, so the decision came down to a few factors and just a good feeling. All three were well qualified, and each had slightly different strengths. I told my client I would be comfortable working with any of them, or even hiring any of the three to design a house for me. The selection of the architect was influenced by the selection of the builder, but the selection of the builder was influenced by the selection of the architect. In the end it was the combination we felt would make the best team.

Building Systems

One other parallel effort we did was to look at building systems. The client and I had discussed Structural Insulated Panels (SIP), Insulated Concrete Form (ICF), and Advanced Framing Systems (AFS) as our preferred methods. My experience showed SIP and AFS to be less expensive than ICF, and our builder interviews confirmed that observation. I researched building systems and found one other potential architect path. One of the SIP suppliers could also act as the project architect, so this gave us one other decision path to consider. One interesting feedback from most of the builders and architects was a preference for AFS. Some of the concerns for SIP and ICF was finding qualified suppliers and installers. This is a valid concern, and I covered this issue in my supply chain section. However, if we want to improve, sometimes we must take calculated risks and put in some extra work to help train the workforce on the latest technologies and improved systems.

The important thing to note about this is the process. It's a little messy to consider several builders, designers, and systems, but this is an important thing to get right. The best design would come from the client, designer, builder, and system supplier working together to optimize the layout and plan.

Various builders and designers had their favorites and biases, and it's important to listen to all of those. I had my own personal biases from building my own home twenty years earlier. My job was to help my client sort through the various claims and understand the pluses and minuses of each approach and supplier.

Water

Most of the efficiency focus until now has been energy related. However, water availability is becoming an issue in many areas. Water cost is usually a fraction of energy costs, so it is sometimes neglected. But water is more fundamental to our survival than energy. Just as with energy, there are many steps you can take to use water much more efficiently. Interestingly, there is also a tightly coupled relationship between water and energy. A large volume of water is used to make energy, so being energy efficient and using renewable energy indirectly saves water. Conversely, acquiring and treating water and treating waste water can be energy intensive, so saving water also saves energy.

Landscaping

I've always been puzzled by our acceptance of developers who strip away the native vegetation from a site, bring in soil with little organic content, plant non-native grass and plants, then leave the homeowner to spend much of their weekend tending to these lawns.

Towns have noise ordinances, but they exempt the lawn equipment that buzzes and screams all weekend. Air quality is an issue in many places, but lawn maintenance equipment spews pollutants at much greater levels than a car with emission controls. Manicured lawns reduce the quality of life in many areas.

Towns even pass ordinances that say your grass has to be cut at a certain height—hence the need for a noise exemption for lawn equipment. I don't understand why some people irrigate so much it causes them to have to mow more often. Spending money to waste water resources so you can do extra work, pollute the air, and annoy your neighbors with noise doesn't seem like a sane path. Put that lawn space and water to good use by growing some food, though some cities have tried to ban people from growing food on their own land.

Imagine a different path. Preserve the native plants and trees. Plant native and well-adapted plants where areas had to be disturbed. Water them only enough to get established, then let them survive on what nature provides. Don't mow, or only mow a few times per year. Grow less lawn and more food. Plant native and adapted trees and ornamental plants. Grow a forest. Enjoy a quiet weekend with minimal lawn work required. That's an enjoyable, integrated solution to a problem we've created.

We left our landscape native and enjoy an amazing array of birds and wildlife. We even set up a trail camera on the property to capture all the creatures of the night. I have a few of my favorite photos posted from a link on my house web site: https://enerjazz.com/house

Energy's Use of Water

Fossil fuel and nuclear power plants use water for cooling. Sometimes it is direct cooling and sometimes it is through evaporation. Central energy plants are very large users of water. Renewable energy uses very little, if any water.

You might think a hydroelectric dam is water efficient. It's just holding some of the river water flow back and directing it through turbines to generate power. But a hydroelectric plant uses more water per unit of energy production than any other method, and it's not even close to the second-place user. It's not the water flowing through the turbine that is lost—that moves downstream. The large surface areas created by the dam dramatically increase the evaporation and loss of water in the river system. Some of that evaporated water may fall back as rain in the river basin, but often it drifts out of that basin and falls elsewhere. The dams also disrupt the natural river ecology.

Some may argue the dams created reservoirs that also provide water for consumption and recreation. They do, but the additional evaporation issue is still a concern. Move upstream, not in the water, but in the consumption process and work on water efficiency. That's where you'll find the most economic and environmentally friendly solution.

Water Saving at Home

Like energy, saving water is an integrative design process. Landscape irrigation is the largest use of water for most homes. Instead of scraping a lot clean and starting from scratch, try to preserve as much of the native grass and trees as possible. Protect the tree root zone during construction. Then, when you install new plants only use native and adapted species. You will likely need some supplemental irrigation to get them established, but if you have the right plants you can ween them off of supplemental irrigation. Also, consider using some of your lawn for growing food.

I'm not sure where the idea originated we should spend a large portion of our weekends mowing, edging, and trimming grass over and over again. Then you have to purchase and maintain all the equipment to do those tasks. Add in the noise and air pollution from lawn equipment, and it appears to be one of the worst habits we've developed. Stop it. Develop a new, better habit—and habitat.

Develop a new, better habit—and habitat.

Native grasses, plants, trees, and food crops are better for us, for nature, and our quality of life. And the natives will reduce your water use.

To water that garden producing your food, you can collect rainwater from your roof (in most locations). I'll move back to the integrative design topic for a minute to talk about the roof. When we chose a metal galvalume roof, it had several benefits already identified: energy efficient, long life, hail resistant, and easy to attach solar panels. It also is great for rainwater collection. Traditional asphalt shingles shed granules and leach byproducts. The galvalume roof is a clean surface to collect rainfall from. Remember the earlier expression, you know you are on the right track when your solution for one problem accidentally solves several others.

Rain collection is governed by just a few simple guidelines. First is the amount of rain you can get from the rainfall in your area. For every 1,000 square feet of roof you can collect 600 gallons with every one inch of rain that falls (0.6 gallons/inch per sf of roof). If you had a 2,000 square foot roof and your area received 25" of rain, then you could collect up to 30,000 gallons in a year (2000 sf x 0.6 gal/in*sf x 25 inches = 30,000 gallons). That doesn't mean you'll need 30,000 gallons of storage, because you'll use up some of the collected water. To size your storage, you really need to look at the rainfall patterns and your water usage season. If you mostly use water in the spring and summer, then the rainfall pattern and amount during that period will be of most importance. We have two 1,600-gallon tanks for a total of 3,200 gallons. We have enough roof draining to the tanks that one inch of rain adds about 1,000 gallons. The water is only used for a small garden and to refill a decorative outdoor pond.

If you have long dry spells you'll need more storage than if your rain is fairly distributed through the year.

Fixture Selection

Selecting a water-efficient fixture is not a sacrifice. Many perform better than their wasteful counterparts. Water sense labeled fixtures are a great start, but even among those labeled fixtures there is a range of efficiency. Make sure to compare actual data between your top few choices. When researching toilets for our home, I found a study that had used fake poo to test the actual one-flush clearing ability of low-flow toilets. They tested a large number of toilets, and one of the best at clearing with one flush was also one of the most affordable. High price doesn't always mean better performance.

It's Black and Grey

Instead of sending everything down a drain to a municipal sewer system or septic field, you can separate your waste water into black water (from toilets) and grey water (from everything else). Grey water can be used to flush toilets and/or provide lawn or garden irrigation.

Another alternative for the black water waste is to eliminate it with an alternate toilet, such as a composting toilet.

By reducing our water, use we've also reduced the energy use of treating and delivering that water. By reducing the energy needed to treat and deliver water, we've reduced the amount of water needed to produce that energy. It's a cascade of efficiency.

When we were choosing our system, we decided since the municipal water supply was so close we would tap that for the interior uses and install rainwater collection for exterior uses only. Our native landscape doesn't need supplemental water, so the rainwater is used for the small vegetable garden and to refill a decorative pond on our property. Our efficient use indoors has kept our average water use very low.

The Supply Chain and Builder

To build better houses we need a support network. You need someone who knows how to design it (in an integrated manner) and someone who knows who to build it—properly. And you need good suppliers for all the components. I freely share our design ideas and systems because I want the companies who design better products and systems to succeed. It helps all of us when we have better choices available, and the suppliers can reduce costs when they are able to scale their products.

I was my own architect and engineer and spent a lot of time optimizing the design, but I had a day job and needed a good builder to be on site managing the construction. Searching for a builder was the one time in the project I almost gave up. I struggled to find someone who understood my vision. I kept talking to builders who would look at my plans with a look of bewilderment and say in their thick Texas accent, "What do you want to do all that for, I'll build you a nice stick house." I eventually hired a guy who said all the right things, but immediately started work without bidding or my authorization. He was quickly fired, and my search resumed.

The US postal service delivered a builder solution for me one day. The *Solar Today* May/June issue from 1994 had an article about a company (BBH Enterprises) that was building energy efficient homes for low-income families—because who needs a low energy bill more than a low-income family? I enjoyed reading the story, then noticed the company was located right here in the Dallas-Ft. Worth area. Being 1994, I picked up the phone book and looked them up in the yellow pages. It was a husband and wife team, Richard and Barbara Harwood. I called and spoke with Richard. I complimented them on the article and asked if they built custom homes. He said he used to back in Chicago, but had been focusing on these low-income family projects recently. I told him a little about my ideas, and he invited me to their house to look at my plans.

We arrived and spread the drawings on their dining room table. After only talking about my plans for what seemed like less than a minute, Richard leaned, clasped his hands, and said, "Please let me build this house for you. This is right in line with what we are already doing, and I'll do a great job for you and look forward to even learning something new." Richard was in his 60s, but had the youthful energy of a person half his age.

We were a perfect match. There's an old saying in the building industry: "Cost, schedule, quality—pick two." I told Richard we had a roof over our head and were in no rush. We wanted the quality to be the top priority, and we needed to take our time and make sure the cost stayed within budget. Builders are schedule-driven people, and Richard did a great job of overcoming that schedule-driven tendency and staying with the priority order. We set up the contract as an open checkbook, cost-plus arrangement. We reviewed the bids together and adjusted and rebid as necessary. Often, we would seek the advice of contractors on how the design could be improved for higher quality and/or lower cost. I approved all the invoices at the end of each month.

Richard was on the job every minute. He would sometimes call me at work with a question. He would put the subcontractor on the phone and have me explain it, then Richard would get on the phone after the sub had walked away and say, "Tell me exactly what you told him so I can follow him and make sure he does it right."

Halfway through my house construction, the BBH Enterprises sign came down and the Enviro Custom Homes sign went up. A new business was born. Enviro Custom Homes went on to build a number of efficient houses in the DFW area.

When we were interviewing architects for my client's house in 2017, we were down to three really good architects. All three were well versed in building science and sustainability, and one of them said something that sums up the supply chain issue. He said, "You never want to be the first to try a new system." If no one tries a new system, then we'll never advance. Someone has to take the risk. It can be a well-studied and calculated risk, but someone has to be the doivist. And they might have to put in a little extra effort to insure it's successful. And then they need to share the idea so others join in. That's how innovative approaches and products become more standardized. That's how appliances reach critical volume to scale up and achieve volume cost efficiency.

A builder once told me, "Why would I want to do anything different? As long as people are buying what I build I don't need to change." Indeed, part of the issue is educated consumers need to demand better products and solutions. You need to walk away from those who do just enough to get by and run toward those who are striving to do better.

Sustainability/Resilience

Energy and water use represent the largest impact our homes have on the environment and planet, but there are a host of other areas where we can make better choices that have less impact on the planet. It belongs in a discussion about efficiency because it's important we also use our resources efficiently. We're an ever-growing population on a finite-sized planet. It took 200,000 years for the human population to reach one billion. It then took about 150 years to triple that to three billion by 1960. It then doubled to six billion in less than forty years. We've now passed seven billion people on the planet.

Now, I'm sure most of them are nice people. They just want shelter, food, and water. And if they aspire to be like the rest of the developed world, we'll find ourselves a couple of planets short of resources. We must find a way to be much more efficient with our use of the planet's resources if we have any hope of supporting this enormous population.

Material Selection

All materials require energy and water to produce, and they often have emissions and pollution issues associated with their production. These can be complex calculations, and there are several organizations attempting to quantify these things. This data should not be the sole driver of any decision, but should be a valuable part of your materials selection process. You'll have to balance production impacts with the material cost, life, functionality, and other factors. If the building is built to have a very long life, then the embodied energy of the materials will be spread over more years, which lessens the net impact.

A term you might encounter for material assessment is Life Cycle Analysis (LCA). The LCA is an attempt to assess the environmental impact of a material through all stages of its life cycle.

Embodied Energy

For a typical home with little attention paid to energy efficiency, the embodied energy of all the materials used to build it might add to about 10% of the total energy (embedded + operating). For an energy-efficient home, that same level of embodied energy might represent 35% of the total. For a passive solar home, the majority of the energy impact could be from the embodied energy. Granted, an efficient home probably uses less overall energy (operating +

embodied), but the embodied energy becomes a larger share of that total energy use and warrants some thought.

Recycled Content

Most people understand recycling is a good way to keep material out of the landfill. It's usually more energy efficient to recycle material than to produce it from scratch. If we are going to recycle effectively, we need a demand for the products made from recycled materials. It's important to look for these opportunities when choosing materials for your home.

Indoor Air Quality

Many materials are made with volatile organic compounds (VOCs) or other chemicals that will off-gas odors into your home. A good example is the "new car smell." People like that smell, but probably not because it's pleasant. It's certainly not good for your health. People like it because they associate it with a new car. In your home, you should choose materials with zero or very low levels of VOC. This applies to paint, adhesives, sealants, coatings, and finishes. Wood products should be screened for formaldehyde. This is particularly common in pressed wood products used in low-cost cabinets. Fortunately, rating systems such as LEED and Greenguard have been working to raise awareness, set standards, and improve the availability of quality products.

Material Source

When choosing any wood for the home, you should make sure it is durable and sustainably sourced. The Forest Stewardship Council (FSC) requires chain of custody documents so you can know where the wood was harvested and milled. Choosing from a reputable supplier helps ensure proper forestry practices were used and the wood was not illegally harvested.

Flooring

If I were building another home I would consider just installing a quality slab pour and go with raw concrete for the flooring. It's cost effective—you were already pouring it for the slab, and now you don't need to buy something to install over it. Flooring choice often depends on the use of the space. Heavily trafficked or water prone areas might receive a different choice than a bedroom.

There are many flooring choices, and among each type there is a range of environmental friendliness. In the world of carpeting, most of it used to be a disposable product. Much of it was made from petrochemicals and thrown in the landfill at the end of life. There are now carpets made from recycled plastic. There are also take back and recycling programs for carpeting. Carpet tiles, which originated as a commercial product, are now available for residential use. You can easily replace a single stained or damaged tile instead of the entire carpet.

Among wood flooring, there are sustainably harvested wood products. There are also reused/salvaged wood floors. Cork is sustainably harvested from the bark of trees. Bamboo, which is really a fast-growing grass, can make a great flooring material. It grows very fast, which means it can be quickly replenished. And it is harder and more durable than other wood products.

Old-fashioned linoleum is a very environmentally friendly flooring material. It's also durable. It is made from linseed oil, pine rosin, ground cork dust, wood flour, and mineral fillers such as calcium carbonate. The backing is often burlap or canvas.

Our two favorite floor materials in our home are the linoleum floor in the kitchen and our bamboo flooring.

Westbrook House Performance and Payback

The assumption is that doing things better will cost more—and that might be true for initial cost, but if you look at the long-term cost it's often best to pay a little more initially for something that will perform better and last longer. It's less expensive in the long term. If you follow the integrative design approach you can minimize that initial cost difference as well. We spent more on the SIP system, which provided much better insulation and reduced infiltration. We bought better windows, which did the same. We installed solar water heating. We purchased an extremely efficient air conditioning system, though it was a smaller system since we reduced the need with the previous steps. Sometimes the initial cost can even be less, so don't just assume it will cost more.

Our contract with the builder was cost plus. We paid the invoices directly and a fee to the builder for project management. We looked at the bids together and updated the cost estimates each month. If necessary, we stopped and tweaked the design or rebid if something looked out of line. And in one case, it really saved us money. As I was looking at the bids and comparing them to typical construction cost data, the drywall and painting bid looked out of line—much higher than I would have expected.

I asked our builder about it, and he said he had just asked for pricing from a contractor who worked on many jobs and always had the lowest bid and did good work. We decided we would go out for competitive bids and make sure we pointed out the ease of installation on the SIP system—there is no hunting for a stud, you can just screw the drywall anywhere as there is 5/8" OSB covering the interior side of every panel. That should speed up their work. The bids came back, and another supplier won with a price that was half of the original bid.

When all was done the house was right at our budget, $87/sf (1996 $). And what was the payback for our sustainability and efficiency efforts? One month.

"Wait, one month?" you may be thinking—"that can't be correct." It is correct from a cash flow standpoint. Think of it this way: I added up the extra we spent on a better envelope, efficient HVAC, and solar water heating. It totaled $13,000. If you put that on the mortgage you can calculate the extra payment. We had a 15-year loan at 5.5%, so we financed the efficiency for $106/month. Mortgage interest is deductible. At a 15% tax rate that's

$8/month in savings. The next cost to finance was $106-$8=$98/month. Note, a 30-year mortgage would have had an even lower monthly cost (but taking much longer to pay off).

After living in the house a while, I compared my utility bills to the average for our area for a similar sized house. It turns out we were averaging about $170/month lower. At the end of the first month in the house, we effectively paid an extra $98 to the mortgage company. We paid $170 LESS to the utility company. We were at least $72 ahead each month. As utility rates increased our delta got more favorable each month. When the house was paid off we got to enjoy the entire cost delta as savings.

The key was to use integrative design to do the right things so the overall additional cost was kept to a minimum. The cost of living in a house is more than just the purchase price and the mortgage payment. Build a right sized, durable, efficient house and your overall monthly cost will be less than the typical path, even if you spend and borrow more to build the house. Four cases below illustrate this. Taxing and insurance companies base the value of the house with heavy weighting on square footage. Build a right-sized house and you'll save on taxes and insurance, not to mention initial cost. Even if you put some of those cost savings from reduced space back into the house in the form of higher quality materials, you'll still be ahead. Building a right-sized, efficient home is the lowest total cost of ownership path. The key is to spend the extra amount in the exact right places so you lower the operating cost and increase the reliability without adding too much to the initial cost. That's where good design comes in. It's a joy to experience truly good design.

Below is our cost data. The original is in 1996 dollars. I've included an inflation adjusted 2018 figure as well. Since I did my own design there is no cost for an architect listed. I show the total cost and the cost per square foot of conditioned space, which was 2,713 sf.

Table 4. House Cost Table

Category	1996 Final Cost	2018 Inflation Adjusted	1996 Cost/sf	2018 Inflation Adjusted Cost/sf
Structural Insulated Panels (SIP)	$32,847	$52,556	$12.11	$19.37
Carpentry	$25,854	$41,366	$9.53	$15.25
Builder Profit	$21,292	$34,068	$7.85	$12.56
Exterior Siding	$18,334	$29,334	$6.76	$10.81
HVAC System (GSHP)	$16,636	$26,617	$6.13	$9.81
Plumbing	$15,977	$25,564	$5.89	$9.42
Concrete Foundation	$15,828	$25,325	$5.83	$9.33
Drywall	$14,769	$23,630	$5.44	$8.71
Roofing (Metal)	$12,154	$19,446	$4.48	$7.17
Builder Overhead	$11,863	$18,980	$4.37	$7.00
Flooring	$11,340	$18,143	$4.18	$6.69
Windows	$6,606	$10,569	$2.43	$3.90
Electrical	$4,880	$7,808	$1.80	$2.88
Aerobic Septic	$4,450	$7,120	$1.64	$2.62
Metal Work	$3,571	$5,714	$1.32	$2.11
Utility Connection	$3,541	$5,665	$1.31	$2.09
Appliances	$3,004	$4,806	$1.11	$1.77
Miscellaneous	$2,839	$4,543	$1.05	$1.67
Permits	$2,400	$3,840	$0.88	$1.42
Solar Water Heating	$1,890	$3,024	$0.70	$1.11
Landscaping	$1,390	$2,224	$0.51	$0.82
Insulation	$1,286	$2,057	$0.47	$0.76
Site Work	$1,125	$1,800	$0.41	$0.66
Out Total	$1,000	$1,600	$0.37	$0.59
Driveway	$625	$1,000	$0.23	$0.37
Fireplace	$605	$968	$0.22	$0.36
Architect	$-	$-	$0.00	$0.00
Grand Total	$236,106	$377,769	$87.03	$139.24

Energy models do a pretty good job of predicting energy use, but there is no substitute for monitoring and tracking actual consumption. I've tracked the performance data since we moved in. Initially just with a spreadsheet and some subscription weather data. In the past few years, I've had circuit-level monitoring to help me better track and manage the internal loads. I recently added web-connected thermostats to get better run data. My old programmable thermostats logged run hours, so I've had that data since the beginning. The solar electric system has real-time monitoring on it as well.

One good measure of the energy performance of a house is *Energy Use Intensity* (EUI). It's derived by dividing the annual energy use by the square footage of the conditioned space. I found some data that indicated the average residential EUI for Texas is 41.5 kBtu/sf/year.

Another measurement that can be used to account for weather variation is degree days (DD). There are two flavors I use, heating degree days (HDD) and cooling degree days (CDD). Heating degree days basically gives an indication of how much and for how long the outside air temperature was below a certain temperature. Typically, they will reference 65°F as the baseline temperature. Cooling degree days are similar but measure how many degrees and for how long the air temperature is above a certain temperature. Below is a snapshot of the DFW degree day data for November of 2016. Data source: http://w2.weather.gov/climate/index.php?wfo=fwd

In Table 5 (next page), you can see there were fifteen cooling degree days on November second. There would be fifteen CDD if the temperature were eighty degrees for 24 hours. This is better than just looking at the high or low temperature, as it provides a more accurate assessment of how the weather was across the entire day and month.

The DFW 30-year averages for November are 282 HDD and 29 CDD. The actual HDD was 101, which is well below normal (much warmer). The CDD total was 64, which was well above normal (much warmer). Later I'll show my chart of HDD and CDD data compared to the averages, and you'll see just how much the DFW area has been warming in the past twenty years.

Degree-day data can be used to normalize the energy use to the weather. That data is included in my data table.

Table 5. Temperature and Degree Days

```
TEMPERATURE IN F:           :
================================
 1    2    3    4    5   6A   6B

DY  MAX  MIN  AVG  DEP  HDD  CDD
================================

 1   88   70   79   17    0   14
 2   85   74   80   18    0   15
 3   75   68   72   10    0    7
 4   76   65   71   10    0    6
 5   71   61   66    5    0    1
 6   70   61   66    6    0    1
 7   68   60   64    4    1    0
 8   65   61   63    3    2    0
 9   68   56   62    3    3    0
10   72   51   62    3    3    0
11   78   52   65    7    0    0
12   70   54   62    4    3    0
13   73   54   64    6    1    0
14   81   56   69   12    0    4
15   85   50   68   11    0    3
16   87   53   70   14    0    5
17   80   58   69   13    0    4
18   72   49   61    5    4    0
19   59   38   49   -6   16    0
20   66   37   52   -3   13    0
21   73   39   56    2    9    0
22   76   62   69   15    0    4
23   68   51   60    7    5    0
24   73   44   59    6    6    0
25   64   50   57    4    8    0
26   67   46   57    5    8    0
27   69   55   62   10    3    0
28   73   54   64   12    1    0
29   74   51   63   12    2    0
30   62   42   52    1   13    0
================================
SM 2188 1622          101   64
================================
```

Figure 24 shows my annual trend for EUI (kBtu/sf/yr) and energy use divided by degree day. The dashed line shows our net use from the electric grid, which is smaller after we added energy generation. My degree day calculations use the appropriate number for my climate and are calculated monthly. For November through March I use the HDD number, and for April through October I use the CDD number.

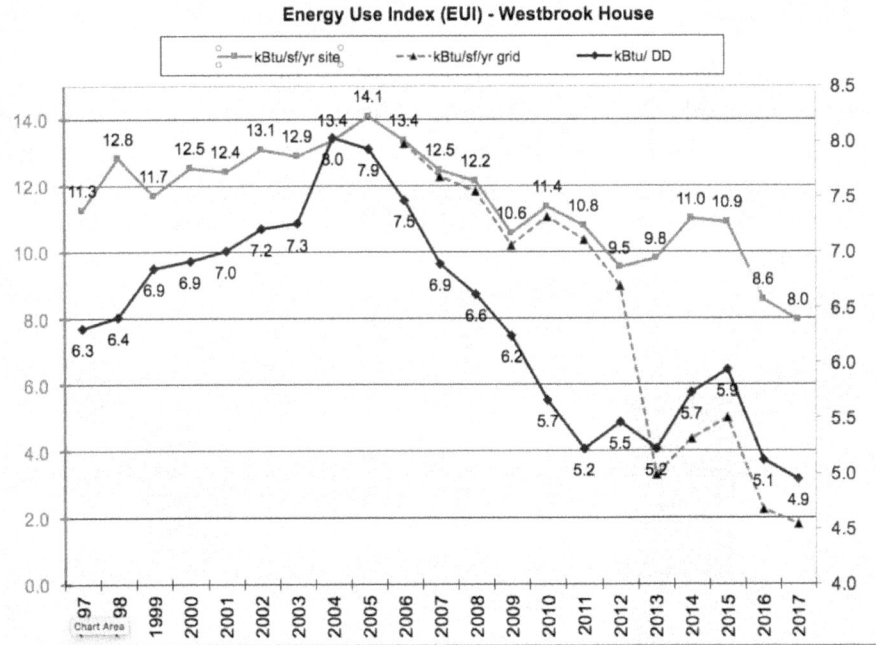

Figure 24. Westbrook house energy use index (EUI)

The peak energy use was when our daughter was in her teenage years and many of our appliances were aging. That peak year coincided with a small leak in our air-conditioner coil which degraded the performance of the unit. Tracking my data helped me note the performance change and find the cause. As we began to upgrade the TV, computers, refrigerator, and more appliances, the internal energy use dropped. Then when our daughter went off to college it fell further. She lived at home for a bit after graduation, giving us one final bump up before it fell to a new low in 2016. Midway through 2016, we replaced our high-energy use aerobic septic aerator with a much more efficient model. This helped drive our 2017 number down even more.

113

Remember, the average EUI in Texas was 41.5. In 2017, we were 8.0. Figure 25 shows how much efficient design played a role in our reduction. The pie chart shows 80% of our reduction is from efficiency. The graphics show our home energy use compared to a typical local conventionally built home. Efficiency measures reduced our energy needs dramatically—and for very little additional cost. Then efficient utility systems further reduced our consumption. This allowed us to install a relatively small solar array to provide most of the energy we use.

We produce our own energy equivalent to 6.2 kBtu/sf/year, which means we are only drawing 1.8 kBtu/sf/year from the grid. Unlike most homes, we also have an aerobic septic system to power. Most residences outsource their sewage energy use to a central plant. If we were on conventional sewer our numbers would look even better, as we would not have to power our own wastewater treatment system on site.

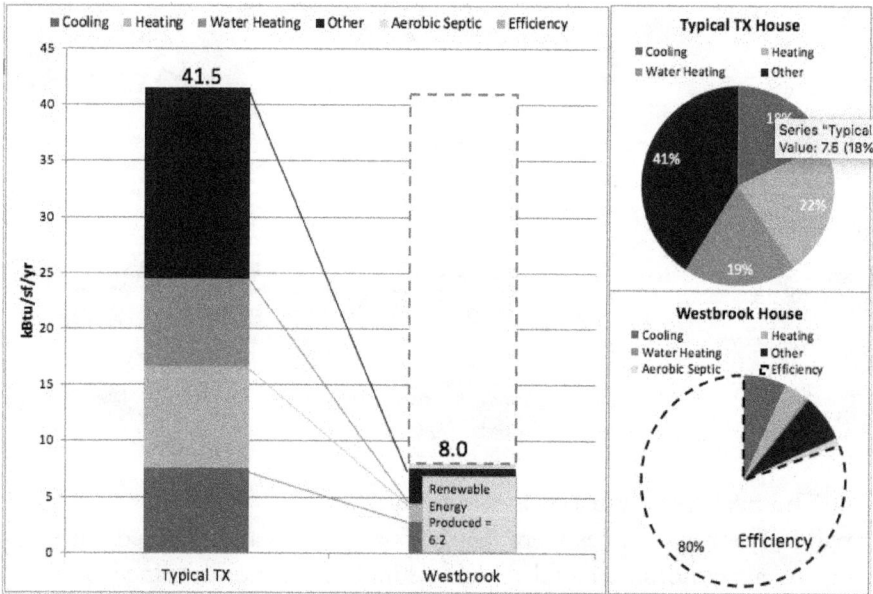

Figure 25. Westbrook house versus a typical Texas house

Table 6, below, is a raw data summary of our energy and water use by year.

Table 6. Westbrook House Utility Use

Westbrook House Annual Utility Data							2,713 sf, 3 people		
Year	kWh sum	kWh util	kWh wind	kWh solar	Elec Cost/Yr	Average Cost/Mo	kBtu/ sf	kWh/ DD	Water Use/Yr (gallons)
1997	8,952	8,952	0		$ 739	$ 61.55	11.3	1.8	34,700
1998	10,195	10,195	0		$ 781	$ 65.09	12.8	1.9	27,900
1999	9,309	9,309	0		$ 644	$ 53.63	11.7	2.0	45,500
2000	9,966	9,966	0		$ 684	$ 56.99	12.5	2.0	38,400
2001	9,875	9,875	0		$ 753	$ 62.79	12.4	2.1	36,000
2002	10,404	10,404	0		$ 893	$ 74.45	13.1	2.1	28,000
2003	10,257	10,257	0		$ 934	$ 77.87	12.9	2.1	38,000
2004	10,624	10,624	0		$ 988	$ 82.37	13.4	2.4	25,000
2005	11,205	11,205	0		$ 1,177	$ 98.08	14.1	2.3	37,000
2006	10,633	10,555	78		$ 1,443	$120.28	13.4	2.2	35,000
2007	9,916	9,770	146		$ 1,305	$108.79	12.5	2.0	28,000
2008	9,661	9,419	242		$ 1,364	$113.65	12.2	1.9	38,000
2009	8,403	8,118	285		$ 1,247	$103.92	10.6	1.8	29,000
2010	9,034	8,788	246		$ 1,222	$101.84	11.4	1.7	34,000
2011	8,571	8,238	333		$ 1,137	$ 94.73	10.8	1.5	42,000
2012	7,573	7,137	228	208	$ 1,033	$ 86.07	9.5	1.6	29,000
2013	7,791	2,625	216	4,950	$ 590	$ 49.21	9.8	1.5	33,000
2014	8,742	3,472	7	5,263	$ 698	$ 58.14	11.0	1.7	28,000
2015	8,670	3,976	0	4,694	$ 735	$ 61.27	10.9	1.7	27,000
2016	6,817	1,786	0	5,031	$ 462	$ 38.51	8.6	1.5	22,000
2017	6,326	1,437	0	4,889	$ 465	$ 38.72	8.0	1.5	22,000
Sums and Averages	kWh sum	kWh util	kWh wind		Cost		kBtu/ sf	kWh/ DD	Water Use (gallons)
Total>	192,924	166,108	1781	25,035	$ 19,295				655,500
Annual>	9,187	7,910			$ 919		11.6	1.9	32,775
Monthly>	766	659			$ 76.57				2,731

https://enerjazz.com/house   2016 major reduction due to aerobic septic air compressor change.

Tips for Existing Homes

Much of the widely available home design information is geared toward new home design, but there is much that can be done in existing homes. It's difficult to generalize about an existing house because the weak points are different for each one. The first step is to locate your house-specific weak points and attack those. The following information can act as a general guide. You can also hire a professional energy auditor to do a complete analysis of your home. I recommend paying an independent auditor to assess your home and provide you with a prioritized checklist. Don't use someone who is just trying to sell you a specific service or product. The roadmap an auditor provides can help you do the right things in the right order. Tackle the fastest payback item, then use your savings from that improvement to finance the next items on the list. Keep moving down the list, and after you tackle the top few you'll have reaped most of the savings.

See the RESNET page (http://www.resnet.us/certified-auditor-rater) to help locate a certified rater for your area.

Some other online tools are:
- Home Energy Saver (http://hes.lbl.gov/consumer/)
- Energy Efficiency and Renewable Energy Site (https://www.energy.gov/eere/efficiency/homes)
- Alliance to Save Energy Home (https://www.ase.org/resources/home-energy-assessment-find-out-exactly-what-your-energy-bill-paying)
- Home Energy Checklist (http://aceee.org/sector/residential) RMI Home Energy Briefs
- (https://www.rmi.org/insight/home-energy-briefs-1-building-envelope/)

Here are some common issues and solutions for existing homes:

Insulation and Infiltration

This is often a weak spot in older homes. First, check attic insulation and add more if necessary. It's difficult to add insulation to existing walls, but you can caulk and seal around windows, doors, outlets, and switches to reduce air infiltration. If your A/C unit and ductwork are in the attic, check the integrity of the ductwork and insulation. Sealing and insulating the delivery system can improve the system performance.

Windows and Solar Gain

If your windows are old aluminum frame models that frequently sweat in winter, it might be time to replace them. If any of your existing windows are exposed to direct sunlight you can benefit from blocking the sun before it hits the glass. Overhangs, awnings, solar screens, and trees/shrubs are just a few ways to tackle the problem.

Roof and Attic Ventilation

Most attics suffer from poor ventilation. You need a high place for hot air to exist, and an equally sized low place for cooler air to enter. Here are two good sources of information:

- Attic Ventilation for Homes:
  (http://www.factsfacts.com/MyHomeRepair/ventilation.htm)
- Tips to Keep Your Attic Cool:
  (http://greenbuilder.com/general/articles/aas.atticcool.html)
- If you are replacing your roof, consider a reflective product:
  (https://www.energystar.gov/products/building_products/roof_pr oducts).
- If it's also hail resistant you will receive a large discount on your homeowner's insurance in Texas.
  (http://www.helpinsure.com/home/roofingx.html)

Radiant Barrier

If you have good ventilation and proper insulation levels, then consider installing a radiant barrier in the attic. Q&A sheet on radiant barriers: (http://www.fsec.ucf.edu/en/publications/html/fsec-en-15/).

Lighting

Install compact fluorescent bulbs or LED bulbs wherever possible. Payback will be very quick, and you'll reduce the amount of waste heat your air conditioner must remove. Most homes will save over $100/year by removing incandescent bulbs.

HVAC

Keep your unit cleaned and change the filter regularly. Wash the coils on the outdoor unit and shade it (without blocking airflow). If your A/C unit and ductwork are in the attic, check the integrity of the ductwork and insulation. Sealing and insulating the delivery system can improve the system performance.

Water Heating

Make sure your water heater is well insulated. You can add an insulation jacket and pipe insulation. Periodically flush sediment from the bottom. Consider adding a timer to electric water heaters to help reduce standby losses.

Appliances

- Use energy-efficient appliances and seek to eliminate phantom loads. (http://energy.gov/energysaver/articles/vampire-power-scary-all-year-round).

- Check the Energy Star database to help select appliances: (https://www.energystar.gov/products)

- Measure your appliance phantom loads with a simple plug-in kWh meter.

- Use plug strips to turn off appliances that aren't in use. Consider automatic Smart Strips to manage attached loads such as monitors and printers.

- Activate your computer power saving features. Screen savers might save screens, but they don't save energy. Let the monitor go to sleep.

Commercial and Industrial Buildings

Work Background

I worked at a large corporation since I graduated from college with my B.S. degree in mechanical engineering. I worked there for 1/3rd of a century, and there were three major phases of my career. The first was as a design engineer for semiconductor manufacturing facilities, known as fabs (short for fabrication). I did system design for a while, then moved into project management. The second major phase was as a facilities manager. Over the course of eight years, I was the facilities manager for three different large facilities. Then I moved back into a project role on probably the most difficult project of my career, an upgrade of an existing fab while it was still operating. Not long after that, the next, and best, phase of my career was born. I was working on a couple of large projects when the story below began to take shape.

Case Study: A New Efficient Manufacturing Facility

The House Story

Of all the stories I tell about projects large and small, the one that seems to get the most response is the one I call "The House Story." We've been opening our house for tours for over two decades as part of the *National Tour of Solar Homes*, organized by the American Solar Energy Society (ASES).

Many of my coworkers and fellow employees had toured my house and were aware of what we had done. Shaunna Black, who had been the vice-president over the organization I worked in, had toured my house and asked me a question at work one day. She said she made some energy improvements to her existing house, but it was still nowhere near as efficient as my house. She knew we had been implementing energy efficiency improvements at our existing offices and factories, but wondered if we could build a factory that was significantly more efficient by using the integrative design technique I used for my house. Not just incremental efficiency, but radical efficiency. I suspected the answer was yes, but asked if I could have a little time to research it. She encouraged me to pull a few like-minded coworkers together and do some analysis. There was no current plan to build a new fab, but it was likely over the next couple of years the opportunity might arise.

There were a few teams that had been formed to do some preliminary analysis for a new fab. They were focused on things like cost, materials, and systems, so I asked if I could form a team focused on sustainability. We dubbed this team *Fabscape*. It was a part-time effort in addition to our regular workloads, but the people who joined had passion and a belief that we could do better.

After many months of part-time research, we generated a number of analytical papers that showed there were very good opportunities. There were many areas we could implement some design changes and realize significant energy savings. And we could make the fab more sustainable. I was in Shaunna's office one day providing an update, and told her I thought we could get at least 20% energy savings by using integrative design. These are large factories that have annual utility bills greater than $10M, so 20% is significant money. She then noted the biggest challenge we would have is how to change our process.

Normally, when the company decides they need a new factory it's usually needed quickly to meet product demand. These fabs are greater than one-million square feet (100,000 square meters) and are fairly complex to design and build. People get conditioned to be risk adverse. If you do the same thing you've always done, then there is little risk of something going wrong. Doing the same thing is faster because you can replicate a previous design with only slight modifications. If you try something new and it doesn't work, you might be blamed, and no one wants to take a large risk with such a big potential downside. One of the semiconductor companies was so risk averse they even had a name for their replicated designs—copy exact. However, as Amory Lovins pointed out, "Copy exact forbids continuous improvement."

Shaunna realized we would need to do something different if we were going to change our design mentality and strive for radical efficiency. She knew we needed some top-level executive support for this approach. As we were kicking around ideas on how to approach this, I mentioned some story about my house tours. Shaunna slapped her desk and said, "That's it. We need to bring our senior VP of manufacturing up to your house and give him the tour. When people can see something, it makes a bigger impression on them." So, we arranged for them to tour my house one Saturday.

There is a parallel portion of the house story going on that involves the Harwoods, who were my homebuilders. Before Shaunna and I started talking about a radically more efficiency factory, I was at work one day when the phone rang. It was Barbara Harwood. She asked what I was doing, and I said, "I'm working, what are you doing?" She said she had picked up a speaker for the Sustainable Dallas Conference at DFW Airport and he asked if she knew anyone that worked at our semiconductor company. He had done some semiconductor fab retrofit work in Europe and saw the potential for efficiency improvements. He was interested in finding a semiconductor company that was planning to build a new factory so they could integrate all the efficiencies from the start.

I said, "Who is the speaker?" She said, "It's Amory Lovins from the Rocky Mountain Institute (RMI)." I was very familiar with Amory's work. I had read a paper of his while I was in college that linked our national security to our energy efficiency. His writing made so much sense, and he was a hero of the efficiency world. Barbara said they had a free hour and wanted to know if they could stop by shortly. I, of course, said yes.

Amory brought a presentation showing some of things he had done on existing factories and what he thought was possible for a new one. He had planted the seeds in my mind that radical efficiency might be possible for a semiconductor fab. We agreed to stay in touch. He came back through Dallas again a year later, and I arranged for him to give his presentation to many of my coworkers. By then we were doing our analysis and writing papers on the ideas, so the timing was perfect. Amory told me about a process they use called a Charrette. They gather all stakeholders together for several days and generate, assess, and combine ideas to rapidly build an integrated plan. We talked about doing one of these for our company when the time was right.

As I began talking up RMI to some our managers and leaders, I encountered a few interesting questions. One VP seemed a bit skeptical, or at least cautious, about this group from Colorado. His questions indicated he pictured us holding hands around a tree in a forest and singing Kumbaya. I assured him they were a top-notch group with technical prowess and experience. Singing was optional.

Now back to the house tour. When our senior VP came for the tour I thought I might get thirty minutes of his time. I gave the standard tour that we do, but he asked a lot of questions—good questions. He was probing and trying to fully understand how integrative design works and how I achieved such significant efficiency gains. He had taken off his VP hat and put on his old engineer hat.

He then said something that you always hope, but never expect, to hear: "What do you need from me to make it happen?"

It was probably about 90 minutes later when we were wrapping up and I showed him my utility bills as proof of success. He looked at those and said, "This is it, that's all you pay?" He then said, "I wish I had come here before I built my own house." Then he asked a key question. "I see how integrative design works in a house, but does it scale up to a million square-foot fab?" There's an old expression about success being when preparation meets opportunity. I was prepared for this opportunity. We had done our own analysis, and I had studied Amory's information in great detail. So, I confidently answered, "Yes, the process is fully scalable, it just has a higher degree of difficulty." He then said something that you always hope, but never expect to hear. "What do you need from me to make it happen?"

Shaunna was standing behind him, and her face lit up with a huge smile. I quickly replied, "I need two things from you. I need your public support on this. When I designed my house I was the architect, engineer, interior designer, and finance department. When we build a large plant, we will need to get everyone on board quickly with a different process—the architects, the engineering firms, our own team, finance, purchasing . . . He said, "I can do that." Then I said, "I need some money to bring in RMI from Colorado and organize a design charrette so we could get a roadmap in place before you approve any project funding."

He asked how much money I needed. I told him, and he said quickly, "You've got it." After he left, Shaunna and I jumped up and down with joy in my utility room. Then I suddenly realized we had to make this happen. It wouldn't be easy, or someone else would have done it already. But we had executive support, a top-notch partner lined up, had studied the issue in some detail, and I was lucky to have outstanding coworkers who could probably pull this off. I quickly began working on organizing the design charrette.

As you can see, it's called *The House Story* because we built our house differently and we shared that journey openly. And that led to a question about doing radical efficiency through integrative design on a large scale, which led to a tour of the house to sell the idea. And the technical preparation was in place because my house builder introduced me to Amory Lovins and RMI. It's a very magical house—and a darn nice place to live.

Just before I retired from the company many years later, I sent a note to that executive VP thanking him for listening and supporting our radical idea. I got a response within a couple of hours. He said, "Best of Luck in the future. It is not often you get a chance to change the way an industry works. With any change like this, it comes down to the confidence you have in the person wanting to change. Your passion, knowledge, and determination that we could improve led to the results we have today. Thanks for all you have done." At the time we suggested the house tour I really didn't think about it in the terms of sales and marketing, but that's exactly what it was. I had to think less like an engineer and more like a sales and marketing person. We had to sell the idea.

Years later I served for a couple of years as a senior fellow for the U.S. State Department's Energy and Climate Partnership of the Americas (ECPA) program. I was visiting an architectural and engineering team in Honduras and giving them a presentation on efficient building design. It was a fairly young and enthusiastic team. Toward the end of my presentation one of them thanked me for coming and said, "What you presented made sense and aligns with our thinking. We are familiar with many of these concepts but have trouble getting our clients to allow us to implement them." So, I asked them, "How many of you are architects and engineers?" All the hands went up. I then asked, "How many of you are sales and marketing specialists?" No hands went up.

I told them they would have to find a progressive client and put on their sales and marketing hats. It would be hard work, but once they found one client who would allow them to implement radical efficiency, then the resulting building would become the only marketing tool they needed. If that project was a success, then others would want to hire them to replicate it. There are many more followers in the world than leaders.

As part of my ECPA role, I visited Bolivia, Honduras, Peru, and Columbia (twice). I worked with governments, industries, and educational institutions on efficiency, renewable energy, and sustainability. I met so many people with great ideas that were doing great work. I learned as much as I taught. I also wondered why, when there were so many people in the world with the desire and talent to build a better world, we weren't advancing faster. Many were being held back from achieving their goals by systemic issues and barriers.

Design Charrette

We still had no idea when the next fab might be funded, but there was enough activity around the topic we decided to organize the charrette so we would be out in front of any approval. RMI organized a dozen experts—some were direct RMI employees, but others were experts from around the world, including Eng Lock Lee from Singapore, Huston Eubank from Canada, and Peter Rumsey from California.

Since we didn't have an approved project yet, I had to guess who to invite from the company side. We ended up with thirty company employees from a diverse range of job roles. In early December of 2003 we convened in a large training room in the basement of one of our buildings in Dallas.

I watched Amory work the room before we convened. When he was talking to an engineer, he was deep in the data and numbers. When he was talking to a VP, he was speaking return on investment and financial gain. He spoke the language of his audience. And that VP who was worried about singing Kumbaya was right in the discussion soaking it up.

And we began. RMI had a primary facilitator—the appropriately named Catherine Greener. And from our company, I invited J.D. Bryant to help facilitate. J.D knew our corporate culture and did a great job keeping us engaged and on track. The sessions vacillated between all of us meeting together and breakout sessions into sub teams to focus on specific systems or issues. We pulsed back and forth between these modes and slowly began optimizing the whole building, not just the individual systems.

The sense of possibility was just electric, and it was renewable electricity. These were engineers who had been given permission, and even encouragement, to optimize something large.

In my 33+ years at the company, these were probably the three most exciting days I experienced. The sense of possibility was just electric, and it was renewable electricity. These were engineers who had been given permission, even encouragement, to optimize something large. And that's what engineers like to do—make things better. Far too often we are tasked with what people think can be done instead of what should be done. Dreaming up a very audacious goal, then figuring out how to get there is where the fun begins. Early afternoon on the first day, I walked out of the room for a quick restroom break. An admin assistant who sat around the corner from the rooms called me over and said, "What is that meeting, what's going on?" I told her what we were doing, and she said, "I've never seen so much positive energy in a meeting. People are just buzzing." She could sense we were up to something big. We couldn't contain it to the room.

Far too often we are tasked with what people think can be done instead of what should be done.

The break-out sessions were interesting, as we would get deep into system design discussions with a large group of engineers, most not shy about voicing their opinion. But there was respect and openness for other ideas. When one of our company engineers would present an idea for doing something differently, the RMI team members would often confirm it was a valid solution, and sometimes share an actual implemented system they had worked on or were familiar with. Peter Rumsey often shared actual projects he had completed. It gave great confidence to the team that we were on the right track.

Eng Lock Lee was often sitting in the back quietly absorbing various points of view. Then, like a Jedi master, he would quietly walk up to the board and sketch out a system design that synthesized all the good discussion. He would sit back down while everyone studied it, then we would start taking pictures of the design. I suspect Eng Lock had much of the optimal answer already, but he practiced the rare art of listening, and he let us work through the issues and come close to the optimum solution. When he summarized it, everyone bought in. It was a diverse group of people with a single and clear focus on doing something great.

At the end of three days, we pulled all the ideas together. We came up with a top list of fifteen big ideas that we thought should be implemented. Because we were in Texas, and people like to claim everything is big in Texas, J.D. dubbed these "The Big Honkin' Ideas." In addition to the big ideas, we had a long list of other good ideas we wanted to implement. One thing I remember about the charrette was we had fun and we laughed—a lot. That kept us loose and open to ideas and possibilities. There were no right or wrong ideas. There were ideas—and they built off each other until an "ah-ha" moment would present itself. It was so good I almost wanted to join hands and sing Kumbaya.

And it was at the charrette we first discussed leadership in energy and environmental design (LEED) certification. On the second day we were discussing some of the good energy, water, and resource saving programs at TI, and Huston Eubank leaned over to me and asked if I had heard of LEED. LEED was still fairly new. I happened to attend the first US Green Building Council (USGBC) conference in Austin about a year before the charrette, so I was familiar with it. Huston said, "You already have some good practices in place, and with what we are talking about here you should make this a LEED factory. I don't think anyone has done LEED on such a grand scale before." The seed was planted, the idea noted for further research.

But the visionaries never give up or linger on the ones that don't bear fruit. They just keep planting seeds.

One thing I've come to realize over the years is people who are real visionaries and can see a better path forward spend a lot of time planting seeds (ideas). Not all of those seeds will germinate and grow—in fact, most don't. But the visionaries never give up or linger on the ones that don't bear fruit. They just keep planting. It only takes a few of those seeds sprouting to lead to great improvements. And sprouting one of those seeds means someone had to nurture and care for it until it grew large enough to be seen by all. I knew what my role was within our company. I had to protect and nurture that seed, and I had to line up enough allies to protect and nurture that seed with me.

At the conclusion of the charrette we got everything packed up, and as the RMI team was loading on the elevator Amory said hold the door, and came out and gave me a big bear hug, completely lifting me off the floor. I think he was pleased. I know I was.

Financial Bombshell of Opportunity

We had a plan now, but the next phase would be a minefield of mediocrity. The opportunity to revert to old ideas and behavior would lurk at every turn. We didn't have a project approved, we didn't know the location, we didn't know much. We just knew if given the chance we could do better than we had ever done before—much better.

Within a month of the charrette, the company approved the funding for the design of a new fab that would be located just up the road in Richardson, Texas. It is called RFAB. But the same senior VP who toured my house and gave us the approval to pursue radical efficiency told us the factory had to be 30% less expensive than the previous one we built in the area less than a decade before. The initial response was, "There goes the sustainable and efficient design features." Conventional "wisdom" said sustainability would cost more, so it couldn't be done for 30% less. However, rumors of sustainability's death had been greatly exaggerated. This ended up being the best news we could have received.

The usual design method is to take the previous factory design, incorporate a few changes from lessons learned, and replicate. To reach a 30% cost reduction goal we couldn't do that. We had to start with a blank sheet of paper. If we were just tweaking previous designs, then all the sustainability items would have been seen as a major change—and likely died a slow and painful exclusionary death. But because we were forced to start with a blank sheet to address capital cost, we could integrate the sustainable items into the design.

The same process we used to identify efficiency features could be used to improve space efficiency and construction cost efficiency.

To get the cost down we had to question everything, and that was exactly what we wanted to do for sustainable and efficient design. The cost-cut request was the best friend of sustainable design. The same process we used to identify efficiency features could be used to improve space efficiency and cost efficiency. And since we were starting from scratch, we could integrate all the operating efficiencies right into the design at a cost savings.

Project Team

Engineers like to deal with science and data—tangible, predictable, repeatable things. Some people are tougher to deal with because they might have limited understanding, a certain ideology, or are even just having a bad day. The selection of the project team was so very critical to the success of this effort.

And our management team got it right. And there was a surprise twist the day before the announcement of the project team, too. My boss called me into his office and said, "We're announcing the project team tomorrow. Are you going to be disappointed if you aren't on the team?" I looked at him skeptically. He continued, "If I assign you to the project team you'll have responsibility for one of the major systems and you'll get focused on that. If we're going to pull this efficient design off, I need you working at a higher level and integrating everything." And that's when my new job title was born. My boss said, "When the announcement comes out you won't be one of the project team members. You'll be the sustainable development manager, and you'll still report to me but be assigned to work on the project." That's officially when the third, and favorite phase of my work career began.

The project team was announced, and it was good. I had guessed correctly on the charrette invitations and ended up only missing one key person who ended up on the project team. Almost all of the team had been at the charrette and had bought in, and the project manager was a perfect pick. Terry Dalton had a good amount of large-project experience. Terry was a calm and steady leader and would listen to a reasoned argument about why we needed to do something. He gathered input and made good decisions. He didn't just jump on every sustainable idea for the sake of doing it, but he always gave it a fair hearing. And we had the data in our favor.

The road ahead was still paved with potholes though. We had to hire the architects, engineers, and a construction firm. And the entire design and build industry had become sub-optimized. They also want to repeat the familiar to speed up the design and minimize their risk, and are often set up to optimize their processes, even if it doesn't optimize the entire project. And that was part of my role, to remind everyone we weren't optimizing the pieces, we were optimizing the whole system—the fab.

I've discussed management, both good and bad, in various prior sections. It's a very important topic, so I'll cover it again here. I'm going to use two terms, managers and leaders. You'll know which one is best once you understand the difference. Managers can't make people be creative. Leaders set up the environment where creativity flourishes. People need to know they are safe to take calculated risks. Leaders identify people's natural strengths and passions and put them in roles that best utilize those. Managers focus on telling people what they need to do to improve. Managers are always trying to "fix" or change people. Leaders recognize the importance of the team dynamic and select people who work together. Managers pit people against each other in ranking systems which lead to competition against your own teammates. Leaders listen far more than they talk. Managers think their position must mean they know better than others. Leaders are always interested in hearing and learning from the people closest to the work.

And those in charge can say all the right things and show all the slides in the world, but credibility comes from behavior. Employees watch their managers like children watch their parents. They will follow their example far more than they will follow their words. A manager who pretends to be a leader but operates like a manager is about the worst possible combination. If you are going to be a leader it has to be your nature, and you have to demonstrate it consistently.

LEED?

After the discussion in the charrette I really dug into LEED to see if it could even apply to a large manufacturing facility. I took the exam and became a LEED Accredited Professional in early 2004. We had several discussions about just following the LEED guidelines without officially registering or going full in and registering for LEED certification.

After much debate, we registered with LEED. I hedged my bet a bit and registered two projects—one for the admin building that was attached to the fab and one for the fab. We set a goal of LEED Gold for the admin building and LEED Silver for the fab—still not quite knowing how we would meet some of the LEED requirements in a complex manufacturing space.

I had really waivered on registering with LEED, but several early project planning meetings showed me why it was valuable. We decided which LEED credits we wanted to pursue, and there were specific requirements we needed to meet. It was clearly defined and removed some of the uncertainly around sustainability—it was a defined goal they could plan around. If we said we want to be sustainable and efficient, then that is open to interpretation. LEED gave us the framework to define specific, measurable goals. With the LEED system, we were able to show people written objectives so they understood what success looked like. We had to be smart about selecting which credits we planned to achieve, but once we did it was easy to communicate to all the suppliers and contractors what we needed to achieve.

Defining something well removes uncertainty. Uncertainly leads to higher bids and slower project delivery.

The biggest advantage from registering with LEED was one I didn't anticipate. It has to do with human nature and competitiveness. Once there was a scoring system in place everyone began to want to know how to score as many points as possible. I always prefer to do the right thing because it's the right thing, but don't underestimate the value of a point system and tapping people's competitive nature. We made an educated decision to target the gold level certification early on. We thought silver was within our grasp, and we stretched to a gold target. Once we got deep in the project, one of our vice presidents asked me how we were doing on the LEED goals. After I updated him he asked, "What would it take to get platinum level?" The answer to that would have been setting that as a goal several months earlier before we got well into the design.

Project Contract Structure

The next big break came in the way we decided to structure the contract. We had the potential suppliers team up and bid together. The construction contractor was going to be the prime, and the architectural and engineering firms were under them. This way there should be no finger pointing if something wasn't right—they came as a team and were expected to work as one. Also, having the construction contractor on board during the design helped identify constructability issues and provided almost real-time cost estimating. Once the winning team was selected we had another big step in the sustainability path: to get them aligned with us.

We kicked off the project with a mini-charrette where we covered goals, expectations, and worked through some of the sustainability plans. This gave the architectural, engineering, and construction teams a chance to understand our aspirations and get involved in the early planning and discussion. This was early in the days of LEED, and there was not a single LEED Accredited Professional in the room except for me, and I was brand new to the system myself.

If contractors are uncertain about something they will tend to put a higher price in there to cover the unknown. We had to spend a lot of time showing them what we asked for was not risky or more expensive. I found most people were very interested in being a better steward of the environment, and they quickly came on board once it was demystified.

We could have done even better if we had built some financial incentives/penalties for meeting certain efficiency and sustainability goals. If the suppliers have a financial stake in the operating results, you can generally get a better design. You can set up penalties for not meeting certain objectives (stick), but you should also set up financial incentives for exceeding the goals (carrot). We did not pursue this path.

Space Efficiency

One of the most critical factors in reaching the aggressive cost reduction goal was space efficiency. John Plata was doing the preliminary fab layouts, and he focused on an efficient layout to eliminate a lot of extra hallways. He integrated the rooms and spaces to really trim down on how much space we needed to build, and, consequently, operate and maintain.

The biggest breakthrough came when we eliminated an entire floor. For a variety of reason, fabs had evolved to be three-floor structures. The main floor was where the manufacturing tools sat. Below that, under a perforated floor, was another level with ducts, pipes, transformers, and some support equipment. Then there was another floor below that with vacuum pumps and more support equipment attached to manufacturing tools. This lowest floor was isolated in a separate airstream, so it required its own cooling and ventilation systems. This design had evolved for two main reasons: one is the amount of support equipment for each manufacturing tool had grown so much it was almost impossible to physically fit them on one floor. Contamination concerns with vacuum pumps, waste lift stations, and other equipment drove those to be isolated on a different floor and a different airstream.

Our fab was going to do a few things differently. One, we were moving to the next generation of manufacturing tools. Our tools used larger wafers (300mm diameter instead of 200mm). These tools were physically larger, so we began to wonder if all the support equipment might fit under them on one floor. Other recent developments, such as stacking racks for vacuum pumps, also made this seem possible. The newer tools were also enclosed and had their own clean environment, which reduced concerns with airborne particles in the general room. And one of our goals from the charrette was to gravity drain all liquid waste out of the factory, which would eliminate pump stations and their potential for overflow and leaks.

Mike Piscopo and John did some analysis and found the support equipment would indeed fit under the tools. And we were able to gravity drain the waste out, which was a simpler, cheaper, more reliable, less costly, and less risky method. Gravity is a very reliable system with no known failures. Pablo Ruiz took the lead on the piping hierarchy to make sure the waste lines had a high priority. Tom Hardzinski took on the challenge of designing the "just right" sized shell to house all these ideas.

Gravity has the lowest cost and highest reliability
of any fluid-moving system.

And we did it. We eliminated an entire floor and the cost to build it, condition it, and maintain it. We gravity-drained all the waste, which eliminated lift stations through the lower level of the facility. That was integrative design in action.

Energy Model

There was one twist in the project conceptual design. Our company leaders wanted to use an Italian architect who we had worked with on several projects, to establish the overall look of the facility, the conceptual design. Their firm provided the concept drawing. I wasn't on the team that went to Italy to work with them, but fortunately a team member emailed back some early sketches. That team member had been in the design charrette and understood the goals, but some of those goals either weren't communicated well or comprehended by the architect.

The first was the layout of the building. It was not laid out with respect to the sun path. The office building was running with a long axis on a SW to NE axis, exposing a giant wall of glass to the brutal late afternoon summer sun. I quickly built an energy model and ran the analysis to show what rotating the building 45 degrees to give it a long east-west axis would do. For the office building alone, this would reduce annual cooling cost by $30,000, not to mention the comfort improvement for the occupant. The next sketch came back with the proper orientation.

There were other things we addressed as well. We had discussed having a large rainwater collection pond on the 92-acre site. The initial sketch had the pond right in front of the building entrance, at the high point of the site. After we pointed out the gravity issue, the pond was moved to the less visible, but much more functional low point of the site. Water could now flow naturally down into the pond.

It was becoming apparent having the charrette where we defined and communicated our goals to all core team members was very important. They were catching things in the conceptual design that would have been tough to fix later in the project. The concept got the orientation right, got the windows in the right place with sun shades, placed the pond in the proper location, and got us off to a good start.

An energy model is almost mandatory if you want to analyze various options early in the design. Modeling is a blend of art and science. There are several software packages designed for energy modeling, and they have continued to get better over the years. The simple one I used helped us get the building rotated properly. We did have to hire some dedicated modeling assistance later in the project to better model the complexities.

Integrating

Just one small example of the challenge of integrative design can be seen in an example about lighting in the administrative building. We identified some lights that had individual controls built in. They were networked together so they could be controlled from a master program, or an individual could add a small program to their computer and control their own light as well. Each fixture had a motion sensor and daylight sensor built in. Lighting energy is a fairly high portion of the energy use in an office building, so highly controllable lighting would allow us to greatly reduce the direct energy use as well as the waste heat from lighting that drove a large portion of the cooling requirements. We had already designed the building to optimize daylighting, so the daylight sensors could just turn off the fixtures that weren't needed. When employees were not in their office the light would also automatically turn off.

When we brought these up, the initial response from the design firm was, "These aren't in the electrical portion budget." This was a suboptimal answer, and indicative of people not seeing the whole picture. If we installed efficient lighting, a reflective roof, quality windows, premium efficiency motors, rotated the building to the optimal axis, and all of the other items that might have a small cost premium, then an interesting thing happens. If you do enough of these, you realize you need less chiller than before. And you need one fewer cooling tower and pump set. And you don't need to build the physical space for that chiller, cooling tower, and pump set. And on a large chiller, that's well over $1M in capital cost reduction. In this case, we spread much of that $1M around to other projects to buy efficiency. The net overall cost was about the same, or even slightly less, but the operating cost would be reduced forever. This is why having a building energy model is so important, to allow you to run the analysis quickly. Shiv Iyer, our electrical engineer, understood it. Our project manager also understood this, and suddenly the more efficient lighting was in the electrical budget.

And the story gets better in far less obvious ways. If we build a building that is a nicer space for people with natural daylighting, controllable lights, and good indoor air quality, then we'll probably have better productivity and fewer sick days. The operating cost of people's salary is usually far more than the utility cost. If you can boost productivity by just one percent, you'll dwarf the energy savings. And in the battle to attract the talent you need to be a great company, these better office spaces might just give you a recruiting edge.

Good design is not a series of compromises,
but a whole system optimization.

Whole system optimization. Ask for it by name.

Safety Factor: Rounding Toward Obesity

Building design teams are abundantly cautious about system sizing. They do not want to get a call several months after a new building is done with the owner yelling at them because the air conditioning system is too small to adequately cool on a hot summer day. No one ever calls them to complain that the system is oversized, which just costs the owner additional capital and adds perpetual operating cost. But we pushed back on oversizing, and it made them very uncomfortable.

In a fab, there are two main cooling systems. The first conditions the incoming outside air by adjusting both the temperature (sensible cooling) and humidity (latent cooling). The second just modifies the temperature (sensible cooling) in the factory. This second system is primarily addressing the waste heat generated inside the building from manufacturing equipment, lighting, and other electrical loads. This is done by running cool water through coils placed up above the ceiling in the airstream.

Rules of thumb might be good for designing thumbs,
but they aren't that great for integrative design.

When the design team gave us their calculations for the amount of watts/square foot (W/sf) of waste heat (cooling load), they seemed quite high. It would have required very large and expensive coils—a lot of copper to purchase. I asked them where the number came from. It was a historical number they used of around 100 W/sf. Sort of a "rule of thumb" combined with some old historical data. Rules of thumb might be good for designing thumbs, but they aren't that great for integrative design.

Some of those numbers can get inflated by a cascade of design safety factors. If each design engineer rounds up the estimate for their portion of the analysis, and then the final engineer summarizing adds a round-up factor for the whole system, then you can end up with a very inflated number. Everyone is busy covering themselves with a safety factor. We needed to fully understand the true cooling load of the space to get this right.

Misplaced Incentives: Supply Chain Equipment

I started analyzing the cooling load in a couple of ways. One was gathering actual operating data from our existing fabs, and the other was a bottom-up analysis of the potential loads. One of the items we had identified was the vacuum pumps. These pumps are attached to manufacturing tools to remove the air, as many of the semiconductor processes are done under vacuum. There can be several of these pumps on just one tool. There are hundreds of them in a large fab—maybe even a thousand in the largest fab. These pumps represented at least 20% of the entire fab energy use, and a large portion of that cooling load we were investigating. We had found much more efficient pumps were available, and variable speed drives could also be added to pumps to further boost their efficiency.

And when we started asking why these better pumps weren't being used, we found a process problem. Our technology is often well ahead of our ability to recognize and utilize it, and that was the case here. Here's how tool purchases typically work: The primary tool manufacturer will supply their tool along with support equipment attached to it. Our purchasing people are always hammering on the tool manufacturer to cut costs. Our management rewarded our purchasing people for cutting initial costs—without considering operating costs. So, we hammered on the primary tool supplier for low cost. The primary tool manufacturer hammers on their suppliers, who also provide the lowest initial cost equipment. This equipment often has a much higher operating cost, but no one discusses that. That's our issue, not theirs. It turns out a more efficient pump had a very small cost premium and would recover that extra cost in just a few months, but we had to make it a priority and request it. I'm sure a manufacturer might have pointed out efficiency issues at some point, but the system was rewarding people for lowest initial cost.

In addition to trying to improve our own purchasing process, we recognized there was the possibility of even greater efficiencies. Since our company was only a small portion of the tool and pump business, we knew we needed to get more semiconductor manufacturers involved if anything significant was going to happen. I had been working with an industry consortium (ISMI - International SEMATECH Manufacturing Initiative) on fab energy issues. This was the perfect group to address this issue, and they ran with it. Working with your competitors to achieve something that benefits all of you is smart business.

We set up meetings with the pump suppliers all coming in back-to-back. They saw their competitors going in and coming out of the presentation room. We wanted to stoke their competitive juices. And they all delivered. The improved pumps were at least 30% more efficient out of the box and could even be more efficient if the manufacturing tools had a way to communicate with them and put them in an idle mode when the tool was not processing wafers. This would require work by the tool suppliers to agree on a communication protocol. And again, the industry consortium was the perfect place to address this issue. These advances are not easy, and they can take many years, but we were pushing the evolution and were seeing good results.

Another common support tool in a fab is a small chiller, or temperature control unit. These are attached to individual tools to remove or add heat and fine-tune temperatures for process operations. Often these units would connect to our process cooling water system to remove heat. We noticed this equipment often had large pressure drops through the heat exchanger, which cost us money in pumping energy. We also noticed they sometimes had poor delta T (only a small change in cooling water temperature as it flowed through). This also wastes pumping energy. If you are moving cooling water through a system, it's advantageous for it to pick up as much heat as possible on each pass. If it only rises 2°F that's not good. A 10°F rise would be much better and would allow much more work to be done for each unit of pumping energy.

One day my coworker, Pablo Ruiz, and I called one of these suppliers. Similar to vacuum pumps, these are often supplied with the primary manufacturing tool, so we are not often involved in specifying details of this equipment. We finally got in touch with an engineer and asked why their pressure drop was so high and their delta T was so poor. He said there was a simple reason: "No one ever asked us for anything better." Pablo and I looked at each other with simultaneous stunned looks on our faces. Then, we both smiled a small grin of opportunity. Once again, the primary tool supplier only cared about small and cheap, as they weren't paying the operating cost. This was another issue we could bring to our ISMI consortium to work on with other semiconductor companies, as improved performance would benefit us all.

Beyond the overall cooling load number there was a question about how that heat was removed. Many tools have direct cooling water connections, so some of the waste heat is removed with water. It is more efficient to remove heat with water than air, so whenever possible this solution is used. And many tools have exhaust, and some heat is removed in that manner.

For the cooling load and coil sizing, my data and analysis showed a much lower cooling load. Assuming we would get some gain from improved vacuum pumps, I had a total of about 60W/sf, with only about half going to the recirculating fan airstream. That meant the coils used in the recirculating air cooling stream should be sized for 30W/sf and not 100W/sf.

This is the type of thing that makes engineering design firms very uncomfortable. If the coils end up being too small they feel they would be blamed and we would request they fix it—at their expense. Putting in larger coils has no risk from their standpoint—we just pay more for a lot more copper and the space to install it. The risks from our side were higher initial cost for something we wouldn't use, and possibly some coil corrosion issues from low flow. After several discussions with management, we agreed to sign a document that said we wouldn't hold the design firm responsible if a coil sized for 30W/sf wasn't adequate. We saved a good amount of money and space using the smaller coils. And I'm happy to report the coils met the load without a problem. It was the right call.

Make people question your calculations and envy your measured data.

It took quite a bit of analysis and integrative design work, and we had to accept the risk. The easy path, and the safe career path, would have been to spend more money and put in the larger coils. We chose the best path. Had it not worked out it could have been a career-limiting decision. However, we felt supported by management and that they were informed of what we did and why. Management can't make employees be creative and innovative, but they can certainly remove the barriers and erect the safety net that allows it to happen. They can't force it, only enable it.

Question Everything

Another area where safety factors might compound is in specifications. Fabs have tight specifications on many items such as temperature, humidity, particles, air velocity, vibration, noise, lighting levels, and much more. These specs often evolved over many years. Sometimes a certain issue might drive someone to tighten a specification, even if that was not necessarily the root cause of the issue. When we began to dig deeper into specifications and ask why, we sometimes found there was no good answer, or the answer was very different than conventional wisdom might suggest.

Consider temperature and humidity. Because processes are being done at sub-microscopic levels, it is certainly desirable to have stable temperature and humidity. Variations could alter reactions and produce unexpected results. Humidity range is set by a couple of physical parameters. On the low end there is a concern about static electricity discharges if the air is too dry. On the upper end there are some chemicals that may react differently if the air is too moist. The safety band is usually a little wider than what is normally specified, so any ability to widen that range can be a big energy saver. If you don't have to dehumidify quite as much, then you can raise your chilled water temperature just a bit and save energy. If you can let the air be a little dryer in the winter, you can save money on humidification.

The set point temperature of fabs is not driven by process, but by people comfort. Again, the process wants a stable temperature, but that set point is driven by trying to keep people comfortable while wearing all their clean-room attire. People are the dirtiest thing in the clean room, so they have to wear a variety of special clothing items to minimize their contamination of the space. And when you cover your body, your feet, your head, your nose, and mouth, and put on safety glasses over your eyes, you can start to get a bit warm. The main covering is called a smock. Some are gowns down to the knees, some are full body suits, and they range the entire spectrum between. Since human error is a risk to manufacturing, it's certainly important to keep people comfortable—not to mention actually caring for people as another valid reason. Many factories ran colder temperatures to help with this issue. Many of those factories are located in very hot climates, so every degree colder adds some energy costs.

We keep the factory cold because people have to wear too much clothing, but what if we looked at the problem the other way. Why do they have to wear so much clothing? Can we protect the product and keep them cooler another way? And the answer lies in evolution. Not Darwin-style evolution, where we let people evolve to tolerate more clothing. I'm talking about the evolution of semiconductor manufacturing. For the first half of my career, every clean room we built had to be cleaner than the previous generation. We were manufacturing tighter geometries and needed cleaner spaces with better specs. Eventually the manufacturing tools started coming with mini clean rooms built over them. Once all the critical tools started doing this, then the big overall room cleanliness was not as important. Then automation began replacing people. Instead of operators handling the wafers, they were now whisked around the factory by robots—and they moved in sealed pods to keep from exposing them to the clean-room air. If there were now fewer people in the clean room and they weren't handling the wafers, why do we even need the clean-room apparel? Or why did we need so much?

And we asked another question: Is the apparel we are using the most comfortable? Can the fabric breathe and still provide the particle protection? Can people feel comfortable at a higher temperature?

One of our employees, Clem Howell, set up a variety of tests in a box that has a particle counter. He tested people in various apparel and had them compare the comfort level. He tested them with and without facemasks. They went through a prescribed set of motions while particulate generation was monitored. The results showed one type of fabric was rated as more comfortable—it breathed a little better. But the surprising result was the face cover made no difference in particle generation. The face mask is probably the item that contributes to discomfort the most. Because you are breathing through the mask it is warmed by your exhale, and that preheats the incoming air. You feel so much better without that face mask, and the data showed it didn't matter.

When we presented these results to management they were skeptical. Long held assumptions are tough to "disprove." They asked if facial hair made any difference and wanted more tests. So, we tested again. The next test yielded a surprising result. A guy with facial hair and no mask was the lowest particle generator of the group. When we began to wonder why that was, Clem noted the bearded guy went through the prescribed gestures a little more slowly and deliberately than the others. After researching the issue a bit, we discovered speed of movement had a much larger impact on particulate generation than any other parameter. It was a real possibility that sloths with no protective covering would generate fewer particles than a fully protected person moving at a normal speed.

As you might imagine, management didn't want the word to get out that employees should just move very slowly. That would be a hit on productivity. Though one could argue slower moving employees would boost the product yield and far offset any slight decrease in speed. Then we had to circle back to our original point. The wafers in this new factory were protected from the room environment with their mini-environments and pods to move the wafers—which were moved by automation, not people. The only people in the room were those monitoring processes or repairing manufacturing equipment. There was also an argument that when tools were opened for maintenance you could expose them to particles from people.

There is some behavioral benefit to putting on the smock. It reminds you to be aware of particulate contamination. You go into the room with a different mindset. The counter to that argument is you can still instill that level of caution without having to put on the extra apparel. And if people are more comfortable they are less likely to rush or make an error due to fatigue. We offered a compromise solution of a lighter weight smock with no face mask unless you were opening a tool to perform maintenance. Management chose the cautious path and stayed with the existing protocol. Also, instead of purchasing smocks from the more comfortable material we had tested, they utilized used smocks from a factory that had gone bankrupt. First cost was all they considered. Change comes slowly sometimes. I used to joke change moved at a glacial pace, but thanks to climate change the glaciers are moving much faster these days. Changing outdated practices still moves too slowly.

Setting Goals

I haven't yet covered our goal-setting process. Goals are very tricky beasts, and sometimes they seemed to be set in a very arbitrary fashion. I think people can get behind a goal better if they know how the goal was derived. In deriving a goal, you need to have enough detail to understand the possible paths to reach it. We wanted to set aggressive goals so we would achieve big results, but if you go too big it might seem impossible, and people would just give up. Once again, we needed management's buy-in. Sometimes bonus money or other rewards are based on meeting goals. If this is the case, then goals will usually be softer. We worked with our management to agree that if we set aggressive goals, then we wouldn't be punished for not meeting them. My main point was it would be better to set a 25% improvement goal and "only" reach 15%, than to set a 10% improvement goal and barely achieve it.

We went back to our detailed data on where the energy in a fab is used. We also had some good ISMI benchmarking data from many other companies. When you examine the energy use in a fab, the largest piece of the pie is the manufacturing tools and their support equipment. They use roughly 45% of the energy in fab. These are the tools we purchase and hook up—and they use almost half the energy we pay for. They also produce most of the waste heat we have to pay to remove or cool, with the biggest user in that tool category being the vacuum pumps. There are hundreds of them in every fab. I talked earlier about our effort to impact the vacuum pump energy, and we factored that into our plans. The next biggest user is often the facility's chilled water system, which is working to cool much of the waste heat from the manufacturing tools. Figure 26 shows the combined contributions of all the manufacturing and facilities systems for an average wafer fab. The vacuum pumps are part of the manufacturing equipment. The chiller is part of the facilities equipment.

Typical Wafer Fab Energy Use Distribution

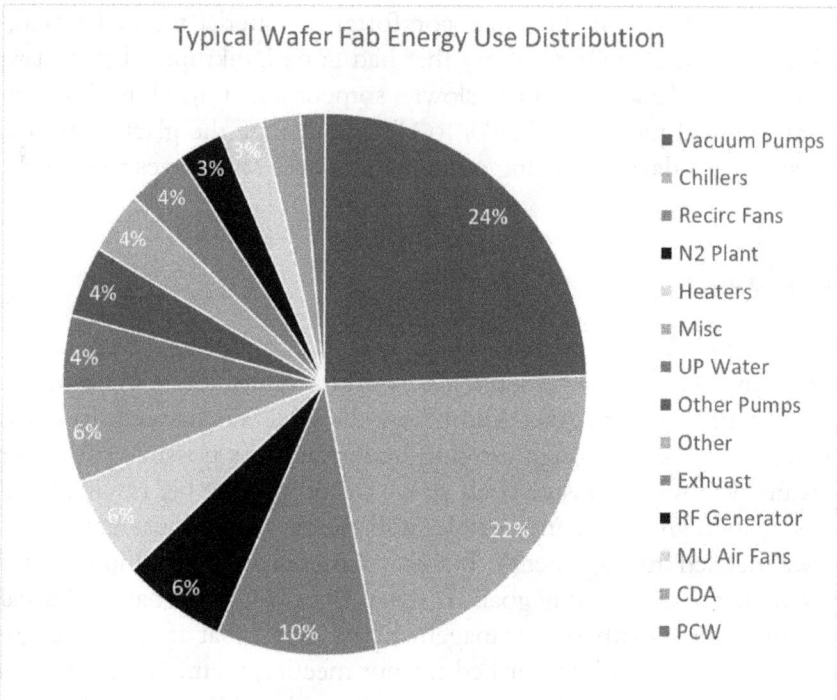

Figure 26. Typical wafer fab energy use distribution. Compiled from various factory measurements and ISMI survey data.

After looking at the data and our plans, we thought we could reduce the tool side by about 10% and our facilities systems by about 30%. 10% of 45% is 4.5%, and 30% of 55% is 16.5%. That adds to a 21% overall reduction, so we set the goal at 20%. Not as aggressive as we could have done, but it was still a large goal.

Educational Process

We did register with LEED, which provided a bit more of a prescriptive approach to efficiency and sustainability. There was still a lot of education and discussion required to help the team understand the goal and requirements. And then there was a fair amount of research needed to help select the right design strategies. I spend a good amount of time on education and training. And, fortunately, some others on the design and construction teams began to get their LEED accreditation. My boss was right to put me in the role of shepherding these changes through.

One of my favorite LEED stories involved a credit for low VOC materials. VOC stands for volatile organic compounds. Materials with a high VOC content are quite odiferous, and breathing those fumes is not good for your health.

One of the materials that LEED addresses is the solvent used to join PVC pipe sections together. The standard was for no greater than 50 grams/liter (g/l) of VOC in the solvent. One day I was sitting in the construction trailer when I heard these work boots clomping down the hall. Those trailer floors really resonate, and a person with heavy work boots makes it feel like a scene from *Jurassic Park* when they walk down the hall. A big guy with overalls and a hard hat leaned in and said, "Are you that green guy?" I responded I was actually more peach-colored, but I invited him in and asked what I could help with. He said, "I can't meet your VOC spec with my pipe glue. I can't put my pipe together." I pulled out my LEED manual to confirm the required VOC level and noticed the can he brought exceeded that level by a factor of 3. As I read the LEED credit I noticed LEED level was based on an older rule from California. This guy worked for a large pipe fitting corporation, so I asked him if they had a branch in California. He said they did, so I asked him to contact them and ask what they were using for PVC adhesive—they've had to meet this specification for many years. He thanked me for my time and clomped on down the hall.

Several days later I heard the familiar boots heading my way. He leaned in and said they had overnighted him a can of their adhesive and he put together a few sections to test it. It seemed to be performing well, and he had ordered a case to use on the job. I invited him in and asked him if he knew why that limit was in place. He said he had no idea. I told him most of the VOC limits were to protect the health of the occupants of the building, but his pipe would probably have off-gassed long before anyone moved in. This VOC rule was about protecting him and his co-workers. They were the ones who breathed those fumes for eight hours a day. We wanted this limit because we were concerned about his health. He paused for what seemed like a long time as he thought, then extended his hand and offered a very heartfelt thank you before clomping down the hall to assemble the piping.

The Mole

When we started the project, I was the only LEED accredited professional on the entire project, including all of the architectural, engineering, and construction firms. One of the young architects from the architectural and engineering (A&E) firm we hired wanted to take her LEED exam, so I helped her study. She passed, and then there were two of us. She could work at her firm to help guide the efforts, dispel myths, and find good design solutions. But her greatest value came as a mole. When the A&E firm would have meetings at their office with none of us there, she would hear doubts expressed about various portions of the project. She would call me and fill me in on the issue and concerns. This gave me time to do some more detailed research and have excellent counter proposals right at my fingertips. When they would come in and meet with us in the general project meeting and bring up an issue, I was so prepared they must have thought I was a genius, or at least psychic. I just had a well-intentioned mole inside their meetings, and it was extremely helpful to keeping the overall project on track.

The mole was an exception, but it does teach an important lesson about finding your allies. When new ideas come forward there is no shortage of people who will speak out against them, and it's wise to listen to their concerns and experience to ensure you've addressed them. But there are also people who will support your ideas, and you need to find them and cultivate that support. It just takes one person to boldly step out and offer a better path to help uncover the like-minded thinkers who hadn't yet voiced their thoughts.

And when the project is done and the new ideas were successful, you should certainly give credit and thanks to your allies. But you should also credit your detractors. People want to be associated with a successful idea or project. You can help turn the detractors into future allies.

Key Design Elements Summary

Now that you've heard a sampling of stories for various portions of the project, here are the "Big Honkin' Ideas" and their final status along with other major ideas that were implemented. I've provided some detail and illustrations for those who are more technically inclined, but some of the value is not in the numbers, but in the illustration of how integrative design can solve multiple challenges and make $1+1 = 3$.

Architecture

1. Energy Model.
Result: We did energy modeling but could have done it more intensively earlier. For complex projects it's best to hire an experienced energy-modeling team. Energy models allow you to try various design schemes and compare the relative energy savings of each one, or a combination of items.

2. Define Site and Architectural Elements using LEED as a framework.
Result: Successful in many areas using the LEED framework. Project registered with LEED and became the first LEED Gold fab in the world. People love scoring points, and that competitive nature helped drive us to implement several ambitious solutions.

3. Passive Conditioning Strategies for Office Building.
Result: We didn't do this for the office building, which is attached to the fab by a corridor. However, we employed passive cooling for the entire mechanical wing.

Passive conditioning can be heating or cooling using natural elements such as the sun, the temperature of the earth, prevailing winds, etc. For the large mechanical wing where the chillers, compressors, water treatment, and other systems are housed, the traditional method has been to air condition the space. This was mainly done because of concerns about the control systems failing in the heat. However, it seemed excessive to pay to air condition 90,000 square feet of space to keep a few small pieces of equipment cool. The building is about 50 feet tall, so the volume is 4.5 million cubic feet. That would be a lot of space to air condition.

We began by looking at earth tube cooling—burying large pipes in the ground and drawing air through them. The earth temperature (69°F in our area) would cool the air flowing through the tubes before it entered the mechanical wing. This would have required quite a large number of tubes running a good distance. We realized we had a very large concrete slab already coupled to the ground and thought it could act as a giant, flat, cooling plate. Heat naturally rises, and we had designed a high section in the center of the building to accommodate some tall liquid storage tanks. We knew the heat would rise and collect at the top of that tall section. The code required a certain level of exhaust from this space, so we put the exhaust fans at the top of the tall section to pull out the hot air. The key to the design was where we placed the grills in the wall to bring in the replacement air. If we put them low to the ground it would draw the hot outside air across our slab and heat it up. We placed the inlet grills up high at about ten feet off the ground. The air coming in would swirl and mix down some, so we would get the needed ventilation, but most of the heat would stay up well above the floor level. The people and equipment were all in the first six feet of elevation, so that was the area that needed to remain cooler.

After we started up the equipment and began generating heat in the space, I waited for a very hot summer day and strung up some temperature sensors at various heights in the space and monitored it for a few days. With outdoor temperatures ranging from 80°F to 103°F, we measured the temperature in the mechanical wing. The area in the elevated section stayed a constant 103°F with no real variation across the day or night. This was our internally generated heat rising to the top to be exhausted out. Down about six feet from there, the temperature was lower with a very slight day/night variation. Another six feet down, the temperature was even lower with more daily variation. At the critical level of six feet above the floor, the temperature never exceeded 82°F. As we continued to add more equipment to the mechanical room this lower temperature rose a bit more. Out of an abundance of caution, the controls team did eventually add a few compressed air eductors to some control cabinets to keep the temperature in those down. It's still much less expensive to cool a few cabinets than an entire mechanical room.

Mechanical

4. Split Chiller Plant – 44°F/56°F with free cooling on 56°F plant.

Result: Used a 40°F/54°F split chiller plant. No free cooling, but we did utilize heat recovery.

Moisture (dew point) control is critical in semiconductor manufacturing. Most facilities use a chilled water system with a temperature around 40°F-42°F to help remove moisture from the air. This occurs when the chilled water runs though the coils in an air-handling unit. The damp air passes over the coils and the moisture condenses out. This also provides cooling to the air. However, it often overcools the air, which then has to be warmed back up before it can be introduced into the factory. Most facilities run hot-water boilers all year round and reheat the air even on a hot summer day. Some of our facilities had installed a "run-around coil," which used a pair of coils and a pump to move heat from the incoming air to after the cooling coil, where it would reheat the air using only pump energy. We would certainly employ this method, but there's another issue with chilled water. Most of the chilled water is used to remove heat directly from the manufacturing tools via a circulating cooling water loop. This water can't be too cold or the pipes carrying it will sweat and drip water—or moisture would condense out and drip inside of a manufacturing tool. The general solution was to use a heat exchanger or blend this water with warmer returning water to heat it up. From a thermal standpoint, we would use a lot of energy to overcool the water, then use some more energy to warm it back up to a certain temperature. It sounds a little silly, but it was a common global practice.

We decided to take a different approach. We set up two different chilled water loops. One was cooled to 40°F and was only used in the make-up air system to reduce the humidity. The second system was only cooled to 54°F and could be used directly in the tool cooling water loop. It takes less energy to cool to 54°F, so that chilled water system operated more efficiently. As I'll explain later in the heat recovery section, there is another advantage to doing it this way.

Since fabs run every hour of the year, they have backup systems in place so they can keep operating at full capacity if a specific piece of equipment is out of service for any reason. Chilled water facilities would always have a backup chiller. Since we had two separate plants, that would have meant purchasing two different backup chillers. That would have increased our capital cost. We realized a low temperature (40°F) chiller could also be a backup for the warmer chiller loop, as it could just be blended into the warmer loop. Problem solved. Figure 27 shows the chiller plant diagram:

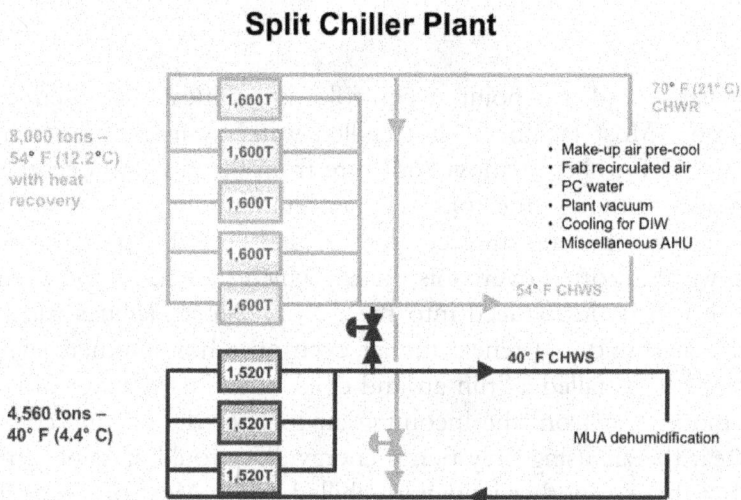

Figure 27. Split temperature chilled water system

Here are some numbers on the chilled water system:

The chilled water system can account for 20-25% of the total fab energy, so it's a major opportunity for energy savings. In addition to the previous steps, we also used variable primary distribution, which means there is only one set of pumps that vary their speed with the demand. These pumps move water through the chillers and through the load. Some CHW systems have two sets of pumps, which is a less efficient method. Here are the general ranges of efficiency for the two loops:

- 40° F (4.4° C) for dehumidification (0.44 - 0.51 kW/ton)
- 54° F (12.2° C) for all other loads (0.32 - 0.50 kW/ton)

As with many good designs, it's much easier to do on paper than implement in real life. There are countless people involved, and everyone has to comprehend the plan, design the system properly, and build it correctly. Quan Hoang was the engineer on this system. He turned the ideas into reality.

5. MUA System Details: Low face velocity, split temperature coils, desiccant wheels.

Results: We used fairly low velocity across the coils and did implement split coils. We did not implement desiccant dehumidification, but the work and testing we did on this project opened the door for desiccant wheel cooling on the factory that came after this one, and it was implemented there.

Since make-up air involves a lot of air movement, it's probably a good time to cover the fan affinity, or cube law. When you increase the speed of a fan, the other properties change in this way: The airflow changes linearly (for every 10% change in speed there is 10% more airflow. The pressure changes at the square of the speed change. The power to run that fan changes at the cube of the speed. Here's a graphic depiction.

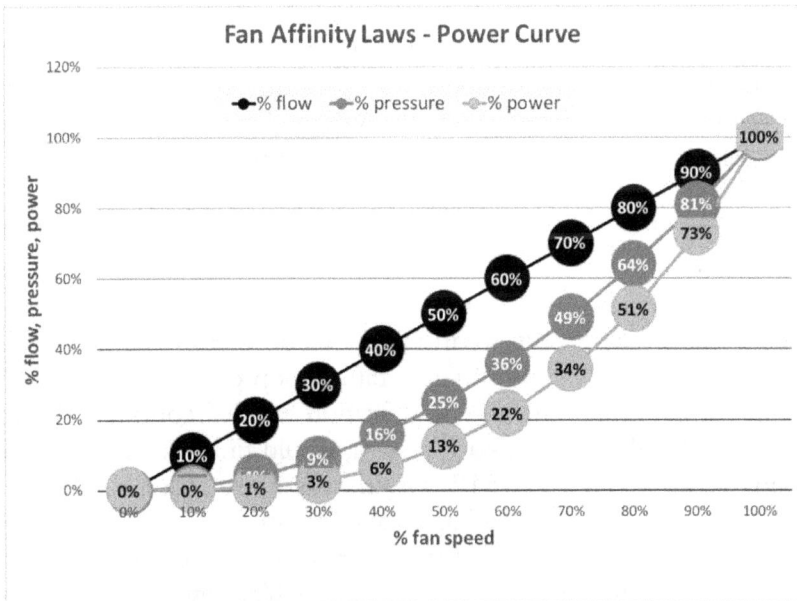

Figure 28. Fan affinity laws showing flow, pressure, and power relationships

Take a simple example. If you have a fan running at 50% speed, then the flow will also be 50%, but the power used will be only 12.5%. If you ran two fans at 50% speed you would have the same airflow as one fan at 100%, but you would only use 25% of the energy (12.5% each). You can see the relationship in Figure 28. The power curve has a cubic relationship to the fan speed and flow, which is why the affinity laws are sometimes called the cube law. This concept will be covered again in the recirculating air section.

Getting back to the lower coil velocity issue. If you can reduce the pressure drop through a system, then you need less power to move the same amount of air. Increasing the size of the coils allows you to still exchange heat, but at a lower air velocity across those coils. This does require some additional space, but not necessarily additional copper for coils. Often, coils are stacked in several rows, so the air has to pass through several coils in succession. If you place the coils side by side, then you achieve the same surface area for contact, but at a much lower velocity and much lower pressure drop. If you halve the air speed, then you'll usually see the pressure drop decrease by a factor of four—and the power requirement will decrease by a factor of eight. You can move the same volume of air with a much smaller motor. A side benefit is now the motor is releasing less waste heat into the airstream, which you don't have to pay to cool. The same thing applies to air filters—increase the surface area so the velocity is lower, then choose low pressure drop air filters to further decrease the overall pressure loss in the system. These steps can dramatically reduce the fan size, resulting in a significant reduction in power use.

The Cube Law. It's not just a good idea—it's the law!

The split chiller plant section discussed the two different chilled water loops. In the make-up air unit, we installed two different coils. The outside air would first see the warmer (54°F) temperature loop coil. If the air was humid, this coil would provide some dehumidification and, of course, some cooling. Then the second coil, from the 40°F system, would finish the dehumidification and cooling process. Since the 54°F system was more efficient, it made sense for it to remove some of the load and have the 40°F system do less work. I'll discuss the desiccant wheel cooling in a later section. And, of course, we used the run-around coils to capture incoming heat (which lowered the load on our cooling coils) and pump it around to the back of the unit where it could be used for reheating the air after dehumidification.

6. Heat Recovery—chillers, compressors, gas plant.
Result: Implemented. It functioned so well the backup boilers were rarely used.

Earlier, I mentioned the conventional fab design was to run boilers all year to reheat the incoming make-up air after it was overcooled during dehumidification. In parallel, fabs are always removing large amounts of internally generated waste heat. What if we could use the waste heat to reheat the incoming air? Since the waste heat is generally a lower temperature than the heat from a boiler, we needed to increase the size of our heating coils to account for that. That modest investment in some additional copper would provide an excellent financial return in operating costs.

Fabs use a lot of compressed air, and air compressors generate a good amount of waste heat. Air compressors run constantly, so that could be a primary source of waste heat. The next source was the waste heat from the chiller plant. This is where our split chiller plant provided another big benefit. The warmer temperature 54°F plant was mostly cooling internal load, which is fairly constant all year long. The 40°F plant varies significantly, because the need is driven by the weather conditions. If the air is cool and dry, we don't even need to operate that plant. The 54°F plant was a near-constant and predictable load. Chillers normally reject heat through cooling towers. By adding a heat exchanger at the chiller, we could choose to capture that waste heat if it was needed. And we could do it on an individual chiller basis to match the load requirement.

A side benefit was water savings. Cooling towers reject heat by evaporating water. If we weren't sending heat to the cooling tower we didn't need water to reject it.

The final stage, if needed, would be a few natural-gas-fired boilers. Our analysis showed this would mostly be used during the start-up phase, in which we had much less internal waste heat. Even then they would only be needed during the coldest of hours. We did run those boilers in very cold temperatures the first couple of years, but once the factory reached a certain level of tool installation we found we didn't need them anymore—no matter the outdoor conditions.

- Heat recovery on 54° F plant (75% of CHW load)
- More constant load year round
- Minimal energy penalty for free hot water
- Reduced boilers from six to two (500HP each)

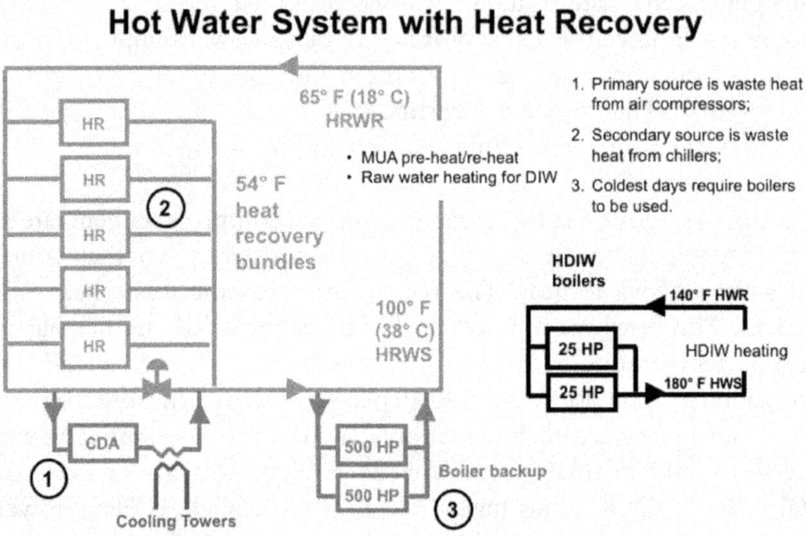

Hot Water System with Heat Recovery

Figure 29. Hot water system with waste heat recovery

Several of these mechanical system connections can be summarized in Figure 30. Some attention to the shell of the building is required. 1.Good insulation is important, but air leakage is the primary concern to address. 2.&3. The internal load consisting of waste heat from lights, people, and manufacturing tools is removed with the 54°F cooling system, both directly and with cooling coils in the recirculating air stream. 4.&5. Many of the tools have exhaust, which is used either to remove heat or chemical fumes. When air is exhausted, replacement air needs to be brought in from the outside. It can be preconditioned using an enthalpy wheel on the general exhaust. In the make-up air unit, it goes through the first run-around coil, then the 54°F cooling coil, then the 40°F cooling coil, then the reheat coil from the run-around system. If heating is needed, then the waste heat from compressors (CDA) and the 54°F chillers can be used with a boiler as the final backup.

Fab Energy Flow

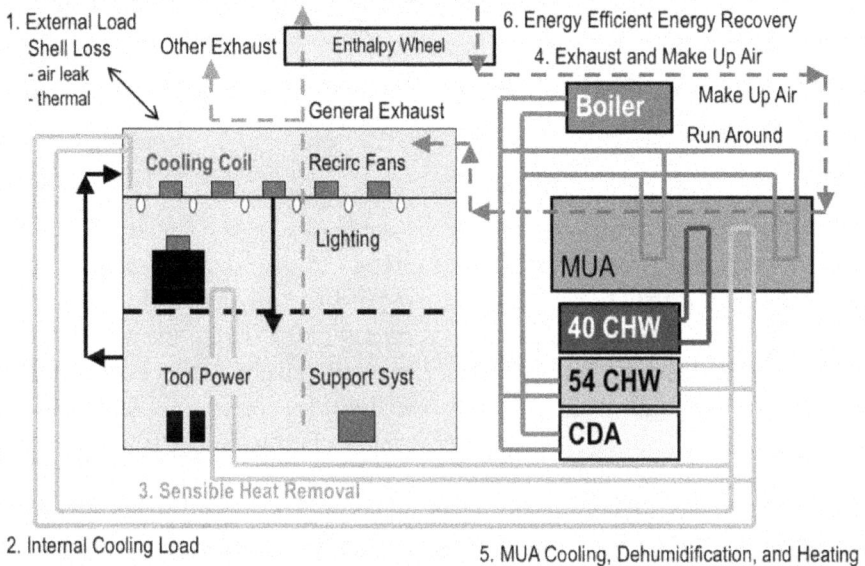

Figure 30. Fab energy flow

Exhaust

7. Midpoint Scrubber Yard Location—reduce run lengths.

Result: We didn't do a midpoint yard, but did place the equipment on the end of the fab, which led to very straight runs—probably even fewer elbows than a midpoint location. John Miller did a nice job designing the system and keeping the big fat ducts running as straight as possible.

This is another example of how reducing the installed pressure drop in a system can provide significant long-term energy savings. Every elbow and T in a duct system creates pressure loss. In systems with significant pressure drop you'll need a much larger motor to pull the air through. By taking time to minimize the installed pressure drop by using short, straight duct runs with minimal turns, you can use a much smaller, less-expensive motor. You'll reap the energy savings for the life of the system, which can be decades.

This is important in ductwork and in piping distribution. One of the areas I think we could have done better is piping distribution. We did make some progress in reducing piping loss in the system, but there is more opportunity available in ultralow pressure drop piping and duct design.

8. Energy Recovery—General Exhaust Enthalpy and Rotary Concentration Thermal Oxidizer (RCTO) Heat.

Result: We left space between general exhaust and make-up air units to install enthalpy recovery wheels in the future. We did not have enough usable and available heat coming from the RCTO.

The general exhaust usually carries heat out of the facility. Because of the rate of airflow, the exhaust stream temperature difference is usually a couple of degrees warmer than the factory. And the air that's blowing through has already been conditioned to the correct dewpoint. If we blow it out of the building, then we have to take whatever mother nature is throwing at us and condition the replacement air to meet our tight specifications. There are two possible solutions. If there is no chance of any chemical contamination in the general exhaust stream, then it shouldn't even leave the building. It's far more efficient to just internally remove some heat than to completely recondition outside replacement air. If there is a concern about potential chemical leaks or dust and contamination issues, then there is still an opportunity to recover much of the energy being exhausted away. One method would be a simple heat exchanger between the outgoing and incoming air streams. This would result in some temperature moderation to the incoming air, but would not have much effect on the moisture issues. The other approach is to use a desiccant material to help transfer moisture between the air streams in addition to the temperature moderation.

An RCTO is an exhaust abatement system that removes any remaining volatile organic compounds (VOCs) from the exhaust air stream. It accomplishes this via combustion of the fumes—basically burning them. This process is at a fairly high temperature, so there is waste heat available. The ability to capture and use that heat was somewhat limited, so we decided to not pursue this idea.

9. Use scrubbers for free cooling.

Result: Did not implement on this project, but subsequently installed this at an existing facility. A scrubber is a piece of equipment used on exhaust systems which might have some residual acid or caustic fumes. Air flows up through a scrubber tower and water trickles down. The water removes the fumes from the air, resulting in slightly acidic water which can be easily chemically treated to make it neutral. The water trickling down is cooled by the air, and some of it evaporates, cooling the air even further. The thought was to use this cooler water as a pre-cool for some process.

Electrical

10. Tool Load Reduction—Manage Loads.
Result: Excellent work through ISMI to work with tool vendors to reduce the raw load. Vacuum pump efficiency improved by more than 30% thanks to this effort. Small tool-attached chillers made good progress too. I covered these improvements and the process in an earlier section.

11. Design to Requirements—Model for Accuracy (Right Sizing).
Result: Good data analysis allowed right sizing of most systems. This was covered in the section on safety factors.

12. Evaluate Onsite Gen/Cogen.
Result: Investigated but found no viable options, or at least no options our management was comfortable with. Cogeneration (Cogen) is essentially building your own power plant to produce electricity right on your site. Natural gas combustion is the most common method. Producing electricity generates large amounts of heat. At most power plants, which are generally located far from the user, the heat is just wasted. If you can pipe it to your facility, there is often a use for it. A negative experience with a cogeneration facility many years before biased our management against this approach.

Process Fluids

13. Use any extra capacity at an adjacent (owned by another company) wafer fab to defer capital.
Result: Did not do this initially but had a plan to tap adjacent gas plant as usage ramped. Didn't implement due to contractual concerns.

14. Phosphoric Acid Waste Collection.
Result: Implemented. The more you can segregate waste streams, the better chance you have of collecting and reusing, selling, or recycling your "waste." Sometimes the output of your process is the input for another, so "waste" might have great value to someone.

15. CMP Water does NOT have to go through final polish loop.

Result: Implemented. There is a portion of the manufacturing process called *Chemical Mechanical Polish* (CMP). It's done late in the process when the chips are less subject to contamination from particles or residue in the water. Most of the factory uses ultrapure water that has multiple steps of treatment. Each step requires energy, consumes resources, and/or rejects a portion of the water. We simply tapped into the treatment stream a bit before the very final processes and could safely use that less intensively treated water in the CMP process.

In addition to the top 15 ideas, we had a long list of other items to pursue. Many of those made it into the final design. For the office building portion of the project, we implemented these items:

1. Passive solar orientation to optimize solar gain and daylighting.

2. Window shade screens to reduce unwanted solar gain.

3. Light shelves to enhance natural daylighting.

4. Reflective roof to reduce the cooling needs.

5. Solar water heating to provide hot water.

6. Advanced lighting with motion sensors, daylight sensors, and individual occupant control.

For the fab and mechanical plant, in addition to the *Big Honkin' Ideas*, we implemented several items. The most impactful was recirculation air efficiency.

While recirculation air didn't make the top 15 list, it was on our list, and it is an important issue to address and another great example of the Cube Law in action. Fabs move air around in a circle 24 hours per day, passing the air through high efficiency particulate air (HEPA) filters. The filters remove airborne dust down to microscopic size. But this constant movement of a large volume of air takes quite a bit of energy. And all that energy also results in additional waste heat into the fab, which has to be cooled using additional energy.

The air circulates through the overhead filters to remove particles and moves down through the room to sweep particles through the floor, where they circulate around through the filters. The goal is smooth, laminar flow with minimal turbulence. For many years, fabs had used 100 feet/minute (fpm) of velocity as the target. For a 200,000 square-foot clean room this would require 20 million cubic feet of air per minute (cfm). These systems run 24 hours/day every day of the year. That requires an enormous amount of energy. Some early energy savings measures resulted in velocities being reduced to 70-80 fpm, which helped, but still required a lot of air. Most of the older fan systems operated at an efficiency of about 2,000 cfm/watt (or worse). The 20 million cfm would require 100,000 watts of energy. That equates to 8,760,000 kWh per year. At $0.10/kWh you'll pay $876,000 each year to spin air around.

Another issue is the high cost of HEPA filters. And the ceiling was covered 100% with them. We had started to see trends in the prior decade where coverage was being reduced to 50% to save on capital, though if the flow was not reduced you would cause higher pressure loss and increased operating cost. And we had seen lower velocities used in rooms with the mini-environments, like ours would have.

And then there are two major design paths for the fans that circulate the air. Most large factories had used very large fans around the perimeter to push the air up above the HEPA filters and pressurize that space. The other method places a small fan on each HEPA filter that pushes the air down through that filter. These systems are called fan filter units (FFUs). The comparison is a few dozen large fans vs. thousands of small fans. Conventional wisdom said the few large fans were less costly, more efficient, and easier to maintain. But the actual right answer is that it depends. It depends on many factors, and some old assumptions might not be valid anymore.

My coworker, Scott Powell, and I spent a lot of time studying these recirculating systems, and we engaged the Lawrence Berkley National Laboratory (LBNL) team as well, as they had done some studies of fabs. We built a big spreadsheet model to optimize a number of parameters. Some of the items we balanced were the percentage coverage of filters with the velocity through the filters and the net velocity in the room. We also had to move enough air to be able to cool the room. We looked at the cost and maintenance issues of the few big fans vs. many small fans and finally determined lifetime costs and efficiency were about equal.

We decided to recommend the FFU for a few keys reasons. One is the space above the filters would be negative pressure. If you had a small leak in the ceiling system or a filter, it wouldn't spew particles into the room like the positive pressure plenum (large fan) method would. The other issue was flexibility. The FFU's had high-efficiency variable speed motors, and we could tune the flow in a much more detailed manner. You can also install variable speed on the large fans, but they vary the speed over an entire large zone. And if you need to add a few FFU's for a particular area, you can easily do so.

Then we set out to make the chosen path as efficient as possible. We opted for very low pressure drop-filters, which still removed the particles, but did so with less resistance to air flow. We had the FFU manufacturers perform energy use tests as part of their bid. This is where LBL really assisted—they provided a testing specification. We specified premium efficiency variable speed drive motors. When we got the bids from three potential FFU suppliers, we had both the cost and the information needed to calculate the operating cost data. This would help develop the lowest total cost of ownership path for this system. We were ready to model and calculate the years of payback for spending a little extra money for the best system. But the calculation was easy. The most efficient FFU also had the lowest bid.

But purchasing the most efficient unit is only part of the process. How those units are operated often makes more of a difference than how efficient they are directly out of the box. Part of our analysis was finding the right quantity of units operating at the optimum speed. Our test specification, along with our on-site testing of the actual units, provided the various data points to help us optimize the system.

The curve in Figure 31 shows the efficiency of the FFU at various speeds. At 100% speed of 1,450 revolutions per minute (RPM) they had an efficiency level of 5,200 cubic feet per minute per kilowatt of power (cfm/kW). At 83% speed that improved to 7,600 cfm/kW. The optimum point was near 50%, where it jumped to 12,000 cfm/kW. However, to keep the proper amount of air flowing, you would have to purchase more units if you ran them at a lower speed. During our analysis of the balance of quantity (initial cost) and operating cost, we determined we would like to operate at 60% speed (850 rpm) and would cover 25% of the ceiling with FFUs. That would give us the required air flow at a very good efficiency of 11,600 cfm/kW (850 rpm, 81W, 940cfm). While we did have to purchase more FFUs than if we had run them at full speed, we quickly made up the capital cost difference with operating savings. And as often is the case with good design, we realized several additional benefits. The noise level was 17dBA less, which is an enormous difference. This provided a much quieter and more pleasant workspace for employees. The other benefit, which we included in our payback calculations, was the reduction in waste heat and the cooling equipment needed to remove that additional heat.

FFU Fan Efficiency

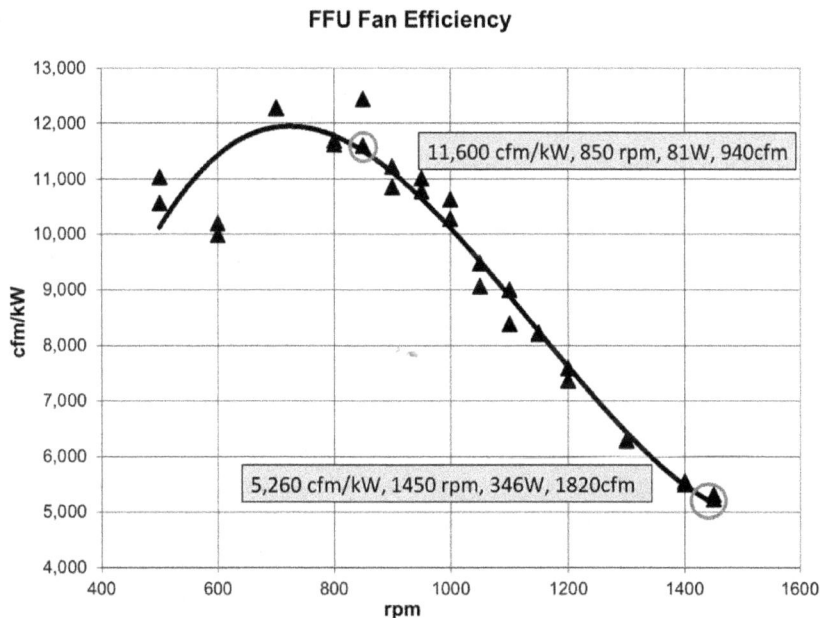

Figures within chart:
11,600 cfm/kW, 850 rpm, 81W, 940cfm
5,260 cfm/kW, 1450 rpm, 346W, 1820cfm

Figure 31. Fan filter unit (FFU) efficiency curve

It was a long road with many variables, but we felt like we had identified our optimum system and conditions.

Resistance is Futile–Do the Math

I've generally stayed clear of too much detailed formulas and analysis so far. I want to expand on the discussion of piping and ductwork losses mentioned in several sections and discuss system design in more detail. I think this is one of the biggest and most overlooked opportunities for energy savings. Remember fan power varies at the cube of the fan speed. The cubic relationship allows for large energy savings for small changes in fan speed. Friction in the distribution system has an even larger savings factor. Pressure loss in a piping is proportional to the pipe diameter to the fifth power (the exponent is actually 5.2). That means if you use a 3" (7.6 cm) diameter pipe instead of 2" (5 cm) diameter pipe, you'll have $1/8^{th}$ the friction loss:

Relative friction loss = $(2/3)^{5.2} = .121$ (roughly $1/8^{th}$)

And the price of pipe only increases at the square of the diameter. That means you should use the larger pipe to reduce friction loss in the system. When you add elbows and other fittings in the system, you add resistance as well. A single 90-degree elbow adds the equivalent of an additional fourteen feet of piping on a 10" diameter pipe system. Material matters as well. Some piping material is fairly smooth with low resistance, while others are fairly rough and create pressure loss.

Another area where I often see poor design that creates loss is in the inlet and outlet conditions of fans and pumps. Far too often there are elbows and fittings too close to the pump. There should be a straight section of pipe or duct before any pump or fan that runs for at least five times the diameter of the pipe or duct. This is to allow the fluid to enter the pump or fan in a uniform manner. Uniform entry conditions allow the fan or pump to work optimally. In addition, the uniform entry conditions reduce wear and tear and extend the life of the components. Note the simple changes in Figure 32 that will significantly reduce the pressure loss and pumping energy required.

Why do we pipe like this?

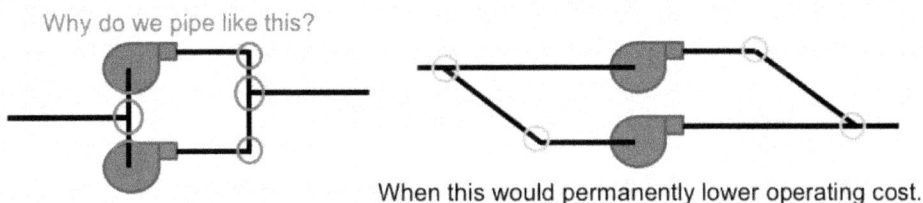

When this would permanently lower operating cost.

Figure 32. Pipe distribution friction loss reduction

If you care to do the math, here is the formula for pumping energy required:

Power (hp) = $\dfrac{\text{Flow (gpm)} * \text{system pressure drop (ft w.g.)}}{3960 \text{ (constant)} * \text{effic pump} * \text{effic motor} * \text{effic drive}}$

Remembering pressure loss changes at the fifth power of the diameter, you can see lowering the system pressure drop to $1/8^{th}$ of the original design also reduces the power needed to just $1/8^{th}$ of the original. Then note the contributions of the efficiency of the pump, motor, and drive system. If you make a 5% improvement in a component efficiency, you enjoy a 5% reduction in energy use.

Poor pipe design leads to friction. Friction leads to pressure drop.
Pressure drop leads to higher energy use.
Higher energy use leads to higher cost.
Higher cost leads to despair.

Reducing the velocity of the fluid flowing in the system also significantly reduces the pumping energy. The pressure loss declines at the square of the flow. And if you are pumping a fluid that is used for cooling, it can also be beneficial to reduce the fluid velocity to allow it to remove more heat with every pass. If a cooling fluid is moving too quickly, it only warms a couple of degrees. This leads to wasted pumping energy as you have to keep moving that fluid around and around to remove the total amount of heat. The difference in temperature is called delta T. When the fluid slows it allows it to warm much more for each unit of pumping energy. You can achieve a higher delta T, which is good.

Turn a fast but lazy river into a gentle but effective stream.

The savings work similarly for air moving systems. If you have an air handling unit (AHU) that is being used to cool or heat an area, there are several opportunities to reduce the velocity and pressure drop. Those reductions cascade through the system and result in significant energy savings.

Design the air systems so they have a large filter area so you can allow the velocity to be low through the filters and coils. Use a variable frequency drive (VFD) to allow the motor to run at a lower speed for the majority of the hours. The lower speed results in a lower pressure drop across the system and amplifies the energy savings.

Sharing with Competitors

Most people in the world are followers. Most don't want to risk being seen as different, or certainly fear being associated with something seen as a failure. They take the safe path and follow in the trails that have been blazed—even if those trails have turned to ruts. And there are a lot of people now stuck in a rut. I mentioned the visionaries planting seeds. When one of those seeds does sprout and is a success, the followers come knocking. And suddenly the baseline is lifted for everyone.

When we received good publicity for our LEED factory, we began to get calls from other companies, including competitors, wanting more information or a tour. We had a long discussion about how open we would be. We finally decided we would openly share our design and process with everyone. We had a few reasons. If other semiconductor companies continued to work with us and improve our common supply chain, then we would all benefit. This supply chain includes engineering and construction firms. When we started our project there were no LEED Accredited Professionals at any of the firms, but there were several by the time we finished. Our support, plus other companies support, accelerates the adoption of new ideas across the industry.

We also decided sharing our design strategy was okay, because while they were catching up with what we had already done, we would be making other improvements on our next project and staying just a bit ahead.

Nothing about the factory design was proprietary. We used readily available materials and systems. The key was the design process. It was how we put it all together. And, unfortunately, that doesn't appear to be as easy to replicate as it should be.

So, we shared with everyone. And over the years we saw our work show up in other factories in a variety of industries.

Tourist Attraction

As we were completing the factory construction in 2006, the market for our products was not growing much, so we followed a plan we had done with several other factories in the past. We let it sit idle. The cost to build the factory with all the facilities systems in place is fairly small compared to the cost of the manufacturing tools. The company would spend the money when the product demand was there.

A few months before we completed construction my phone rang one afternoon, and the voice on the other end said "This is Tom Friedman with the *New York Times*. I'm filming a documentary called *Addicted to Oil*, and Amory Lovins told me I need to come see what you guys are doing. Can I come shoot video next week?"

Excitement and panic set in for me. I was delighted to get the chance to show off what we had done, but large corporations are a bit cautious on media coming in. I gathered more details and got to work on getting an official approval. Fortunately, Shaunna helped guide it to approval, and about a week later Tom and the film crew arrived. We toured him and showed what we were doing. He even wanted to put on a smock and enter the clean room. After a full day of filming, we were walking back to the construction trailer when Tom said, "I'm writing a column about this too." And that column came out a couple of weeks later, and my life was changed.
(https://www.nytimes.com/2006/01/18/opinion/a-green-dream-in-texas.html)

Interview and speaking requests started pouring in. People wanted to come tour the facility. Every speech or interview led to a request for even more.

I went to our management and told them this was starting to eat up a lot of hours. I had tried to be selective on accepting requests, but it was still a load. Shaunna wisely pointed out that eventually the interest would fade, and this was good, free publicity for the company. She said I should run with it for a while.

During this idle period, we gave tours. We gave a lot of tours. From school kids to stock analysts and everyone in between. Which reminds me of one of my favorite features that we designed into the facility. In all of our other fabs we aren't really set up for viewing into the clean room. Sometimes there are narrow windows in an exit door that you can look in, but often visitors would have to put on full smocks to go in and see the manufacturing process. This takes a lot of time, and the visitors clogging up the smock room slows down the employees trying to get in and out. In our new facility, we decided to put a dedicated aisle along part of one of the walls. It would be in the clean room but separated by a full-height glass wall. Visitors could walk in wearing their street clothes and get a great view of the fab and the activity going on. This is not only good for general visitors, but it's great for customers too.

In addition to student groups, reporters, government officials, NGO's, and retirees, I toured people from a number of other corporations through the project. I became a seed planter, and over the course of a few years I saw some of those seeds grow when nurtured by others. The biggest one was a data center project. Dale Hoenshell from Electronic Data Systems (EDS) had seen an article about our factory and called me for a tour. At the conclusion of the tour, Dale shared his dream of getting his company to make radical efficiency improvements in a new data center they were discussing. He asked if I would tour the EDS board of directors and help convince them to try a similar design approach. I did tour them and got them engaged with RMI. I even attended their design charrette and contributed a few ideas. The result was one of the most efficient data centers in the world in Wynyard, UK. HP later acquired EDS and operates this data center.

One day I was asked to tour a stock analyst who was very interested in the LEED features of the factory. We covered all the initial and operating cost-saving features. As we returned to the lobby we stopped at the vertical glass fountain. A company executive had asked for a *feng shui* feature in the lobby, so a vertical frosted glass pane was installed, and water cascaded down the face. The analyst was standing next to the water feature when he summarized the tour by saying, "You have the lowest-cost factory, highly discounted manufacturing equipment, low operating cost, and are the first analog chip factory running the 300mm wafers. This thing is like the Death Star for your competitors." He then asked me about the water feature. "Is this recycled water?" he asked. I replied, "No, it's the tears of our competition." Then I asked him not to print that so I wouldn't seem too snarky. But it may have been true.

There was an unexpected downside to all the good favorable publicity we received. There were several of us that were giving tours—primarily because there were more requests than any one person could handle. But I got most of the media and speaking requests. These were often funneled to me by our public relations team. The company was very cautious about having people speak on behalf of the company. I attended our internal media training and sent my slides for approval during the first few presentations and appearances. There was often a public relations representative with me initially, but once they became comfortable with me they let me run with it. Ironically, it was much more efficient to just send everything to me—and I do love efficiency. And we didn't accept every request. We turned down far more than we accepted. And I had developed a thick set of slides and could easily hide/show the appropriate set for whatever the audience was. I was very conscious of trying to understand the audience and speak to areas that might be of the most interest to them. And one day I got a call our company's board of directors was in town for a meeting, and they specifically asked me to give them a tour of the fab. The things they were interested in were much different than a local environmental group tour.

When I did interviews and presentations, I tried to make sure and credit the team and specific team members as often as possible. I used "we" instead of "I." The problem is, for the interviews I didn't control the final story, and they often didn't mention anyone else on the team.

One day my boss called me and said I needed to let others do some of the presentations and media appearances. Apparently, there was some concern I was taking too much credit for the project. I began sending out the requests to a number of people, asking for volunteers. And most of the time no one volunteered. Occasionally, when someone would volunteer (usually it was for a presentation in a nice location), they would call and ask for my slides—and then they would call and ask a lot of questions about the slides. Then public relations would get concerned someone without training was going out to speak. The problem is a lot of the stories weren't printed on the slides. And the stories are what engages listeners. The slides are just supporting backdrops, and others couldn't tell "the house story" in full because there were only three of us in my house that day. It was pretty inefficient, but I at least tried to spread the presentation opportunities. And I did enough presentations and interviews that I built my skill at doing them—which was good, because I even had a couple of live radio and TV appearances. Unfortunately, the perception by a few that I was taking too much credit continued to be a nagging problem for many years.

Startup and Data

As often happened during this project, our patience with installing the manufacturing equipment turned into an opportunity. When the recession hit in 2008, several semiconductor firms went bankrupt. A large fab in the U.S. closed and had a large supply of lightly used manufacturing tools that were now idle. We were able to purchase those for pennies on the dollar. As product demand recovered after the recession, the decision was made to start up the factory, and the low-cost and lightly used equipment was shipped in and installed. Now the factory was going to get a full test to see how well the efficiency measures worked.

After the long idle period there were some different people involved in the startup, and in a few cases, we drifted away from the original plans and intent, but for the most part we were able to keep everything on track. Early operational data looked promising, but it's a slow process. You don't fill a factory this large with 100% of the manufacturing tools right away. It takes years—sometimes a decade—to fully fill it. But once we got to about half full and gathered a couple of years of data we could begin to see if our efficiency predictions were accurate. It turns out we were off—by quite a bit. I had predicted we could be 20% more energy efficient than our previous factory that was built less than ten years earlier, just six miles away. Turns out we were 41% more efficient. We missed, but in a good way. The compounding effects of our many good ideas kept building on each other.

The way we measure our wafer fab efficiency is a combination of energy per pattern run and the loading of the factory. A pattern is a layer on the wafer, and a typical wafer gets between twenty and thirty patterns laid down. Every pattern requires photolithography followed by one or more process to etch or deposit material. It's a pretty good denominator, because the more patterns a wafer has, the longer it usually spends in the factory. On the

Y-axis we have the total energy divided by the number of patterns run. On the X-axis we have the percent that the fab is loaded—how close it is to running at full capacity. A fab at full capacity is more efficient because there is less idle energy being wasted. If a tool runs five wafers or fifty wafers in a day, it's energy use is not much different. The tool is running while waiting for wafers, the lights are on, the support equipment is on, the exhaust is on, etc. We would plot the quarterly data points and connect them with a curve to generate the fab's "energy curve." The same can be done for water.

Figure 33 shows the energy curve for two factories that both run the same diameter wafer, and they are six miles apart, so they operate in the same climate conditions. They were built about ten years apart. The new fab is operating at about 40% higher energy efficiency than the old one.

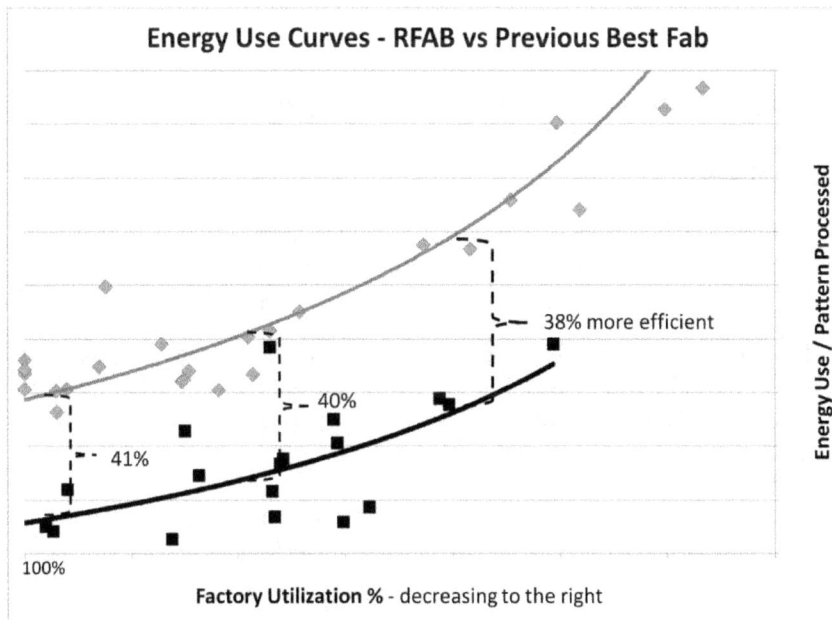

Figure 33. Fab efficiency results

Repeat and Improve

Not long after the fab project we got the chance to build off the ideas. The fab is the front end of the semiconductor manufacturing process. The chips are built onto large silicon wafers in the fab, then the back end of the process comes into play as the chips are sliced from the wafer, packaged into plastic with metal leads, tested, and shipped to the customer. These facilities are often called Assembly/Test, or AT for short. The next large project that came up was a new AT facility in the Philippines.

We repeated the charrette process, though it was a smaller group. We wanted to build off the fab ideas and add a few more items that we weren't able to tackle in the fab. Below is a summary of the *Big Honkin' Ideas* for the AT and a short summary of the results.

AT Site Key Elements Design Summary

Mechanical—Air

1. FFU's variable velocity driven by local temperature. We did use variable speed FFUs, but did not use local temperature to drive the speed. We continued to use particles as the main driver of the velocity setpoint.

2. Desiccant dehumidification in make-up air units. This was one we tried to implement in the fab, but couldn't get the large units built and tested in time. But it worked out well, because the Philippines was an even better climate for this type of system.

3. Include performance specs in design documents (cfm/kW, kW/ton, etc.). We got even better at this. Still not perfect, but better.

Mechanical—Chilled Water

4. Simplify chiller piping, pumping, and controls. We were trying to do better with long, fat, straight pipes. Avoiding elbows and bends is hard to convey to those who draw and install pipe systems. Some progress was made, but we are still far from our capability.

5. Use single temp 50°F chiller plant (made possible by desiccant wheel dehumidification). Since we implemented the desiccant wheel make-up air units, we only needed a single chilled water system running at 50°F.

6. Design chiller plant using efficiency goals (.544 kW/ton). We did pretty well on the design, but there have been ongoing operational issues that have kept us below our potential. It's an efficient plant, just not as efficient as it could be.

Mechanical—Process Cooling Water

7. Optimize system piping design—layout and materials. Similar to the chilled water, this is an ongoing challenge. We're making slow and steady progress, but breakthrough solutions are available.

8. Integrated water use and reuse plan. We did pretty well, and this is an area the operational team continued to work. They grew into the habit of looking for where the "waste," or output flow from one process was of sufficient quality to be the input for another process.

9. Challenge DI Water Specification. The AT site generally doesn't need the level of quality of the fab front end, and we made some inroads. Challenge specifications are always difficult, and change doesn't come quickly or easily.

Chemical/Gas

10. Use closed-loop cryogenic instead of LN2 distribution.

11. Use O2 rich liquid from N2 generator cold box for cooling opportunities and use free cooling from vaporizers.

12. Implement a split pressure and/or split dewpoint CDA system.

Architectural

13. Implement a solar PV system on roof. Didn't pursue. Initially the rules in the country made it unfavorable, and then our own internal upper level management bias against renewable energy kept anything from getting started.

14. Rain water harvesting from roof and parking. We did a runoff collection pond to avoid downstream flooding. The volcanic soil (not far from Mount Pinatubo) is so porous the ground would soak up the water quickly.

15. Natural daylighting in all areas. We did well getting views and daylight to many areas. The floor plates are so large it's tough to get it

everywhere, but it is a vast improvement over the dark windowless boxes of some of our older sites.

Electrical

16. Lowest life-cycle cost power distribution

17. Reduce quantity of ONEACs

18. Establish new standards for lighting efficiency and ROI

Tools

19. Green chemical substitutions

20. Challenge existing specs for temp, humidity, DI water cleanliness, air showers, smocks, CDA dew point, etc.

21. Drive tool energy efficiency—delta P, delta T, idle flow, exhaust, etc.

Note that not all the big ideas were implemented. The important step is going through the charrette process and identifying the major opportunities. Even if you only successfully implement half the ideas, you are much better off than just following the business as usual approach. It was more difficult to achieve LEED in the Philippines because no had done it there before. In the end, this new AT facility was the first LEED Gold certified building in the entire country. Fellow engineer Matt Gulley was on the ground there and responsible for this achievement. The new AT facility was certainly more energy efficient than our other AT facilities, but it wasn't quite the spectacular jump in efficiency that RFAB achieved. Still, it is saving the company quite a bit of money in energy costs each year.

New Commercial Building Design Summary

The major steps we used to build large factories is applicable to most commercial and industrial buildings. The major steps are:

1. Select a good location with the proper orientation.

2. Set a project budget goal.

3. Select the right partners: builder, architect, engineering firms.

4. Hold a design charrette to stretch and align thinking and goals.

5. Work the layout of the spaces.

    a. List the approximate spaces, functions, and sizes.
    b. Consider people flow and space connections.
    c. Optimize the building surface to volume ratio.
    d. Place most windows on the north and south, few on the east and west.
    e. Select window locations and sizes—balancing energy, views, daylighting.
    f. Keep plumbing areas clustered together.
    g. Consider mechanical and electrical system layout and distribution.

6. Perform an energy analysis of the proposed design.

    a. Do a Pareto analysis of all electrical loads.
    b. Focus on the top loads and challenge all rules of thumb and assumptions.

7. Do a detailed mechanical system review to find the best cooling and heating system for your climate and loads.

8. Select structural system and components.

9. Fine-tune the window sizes, locations, and overhangs.

10. Select final plumbing, mechanical, and electrical fixtures with a focus on efficiency.

11. Run a rough project cost analysis as you go—as real time as possible.

12. Run various materials and insulation values through the energy model to optimize the energy performance and cost.

13. If needed, return to step five and make another layout optimization pass.

14. Perform a full cost analysis.

15. Layout or plan for renewable energy generation systems.

Iteration is the key. Everything is connected, and as you change one thing you affect many others. Repeat the process, or sections of the process, as often as needed. The small amount of extra design time and cost will be quickly recovered with a faster, smoother construction process and perpetual operational savings.

Existing Building Improvements

After we greatly improved the efficiency of our new buildings, we turned to our existing factories. Some of these buildings were old—older than me. Existing buildings are more challenging, but there are great gains that can be achieved in those as well. And because existing buildings comprise the majority of the energy and water use, even small gains become large savings when multiplied across numerous sites. We just needed a strategy and a plan.

Strategy

There were several strategies which proved very effective. We weren't interested in building a big central organization of people. Our belief was people on the ground, at the sites, would have the best chance of identifying and implementing changes. I would often get calls from fellow employees wanting to join my "sustainability team." I didn't have a formal team. I would ask them what group they worked in and what things they thought could be improved, then asked if they thought they could implement those changes and what help they needed. An insider has the insight to the details and the internal contacts to help promote change—and hopefully they were a respected employee. This strategy worked well across several areas of the company.

For the facilities side, we formed a virtual team of energy champions at each major site around the world. These champions were usually engineers and had responsibility for one of the major systems at each site. We had monthly web/phone conferences to talk about project ideas and build some working knowledge of energy issues. The champions were the interface and communication conduit to each site. They knew who the right contacts were for various systems and issues, and they knew the inner workings at their site. These sites are all around the world in a variety of cultures, so I relied on their local expertise to take the right approach for their facility.

The second approach was to develop a "Best Practices" list by major system. We began by gathering system engineers from various areas such as exhaust, chiller plants, and lighting, and gathered their best ideas. The lists were developed as Excel spreadsheets with two major sections. The first section was the proposed metrics for those systems. The second section was a line by line list of ideas to operate an efficient system. The metrics would help identify key operating parameters such as energy use per unit of production. Metrics would help identify potential target areas and eventually measure success.

Figure 34 on the following page shows some of the data we worked to collect for our heating, ventilating, and air conditioning (HVAC) systems. Figure 35 shows a portion of the checklist of good practices. We used these to collect operating data and find out where the best performers and biggest opportunities were. For the checklist, each site initially just marked the lists indicating which practices they had already implemented. When we matrixed all the site info together, we could visually see areas of educational and training opportunities in various systems. Portions of the HVAC best practices are shown, but there were also sheets for exhaust, water, lighting, manufacturing tools, compressed air, chilled water, and hot water systems.

Site:	Site 3
Site System Owner:	Owner 3

HVAC (Office) System Metrics

Trend?	Data	Units (IP)	
		sq ft	Office Area
		people	Office Population
		deg F	Temperature Set Point
		%	Humidity Set Point
		in w.g.	Manufacturing Static Pressure Set Point
		kW	Make-up air (MUA) Power
		cfm	MUA Flow
		in w.g.	MUA Total Pressure Drop
		in w.g.	MUA Filter Pressure Drop
		kW	Recirculating Air Power
		cfm	Recirculating Air Flow
		in w.g.	Recirculating Air Total Pressure Drop
		in w.g.	Recirculating Air Filter Pressure Drop
		fpm	Recirculating Air Average Filter Face Velocity

HVAC (Manufacturing) System Metrics

Trend?	Data	Units (IP)	
		sq ft	Manufacturing Area
		deg F	Temperature Set Point
		%	Humidity Set Point
		in w.g.	Manufacturing Static Pressure Set Point
		kW	Make-up air (MUA) Power
		cfm	MUA Flow
		in w.g.	MUA Total Pressure Drop
		in w.g.	MUA Filter Pressure Drop
		kW	Recirculating Air Power
		cfm	Recirculating Air Flow
		in w.g.	Recirculating Air Total Pressure Drop
		in w.g.	Recirculating Air Filter Pressure Drop
		fpm	Recirculating Air Average Filter Face Velocity

Figure 34. Best practices — data collected

HVAC (General) Best Practices

	Check for system duct leaks and repair.
	Check for and replace/repair system constraints such as undersized duct or broken dampers.
	Downsize motors to meet actual requirements based upon real loads.
	Evaluate all motor systems utilizing "Motor Master" software, "Magnetek Energy Savings. Predictor"
	Face velocities on coils and filters should be less than 500 FPM.
	ΔT on chilled water coils should be $\geq 15°F$
	ΔT on hot water coils $\geq 20°F$
	Air filters have low initial pressure drop (<0.3" for prefilters; <0.4" for final filters)
	Change filters based on pressure drop rather than a time schedule. Recommended pressure drop
	Cooling and heating coils should be 10 rows or less.
	Use hot water for reheat rather than electrical resistance heaters.
	Supply and return ducts designed for minimal pressure drop.
	Use sweeping elbows and turning vanes rather than hard corners or taps in ductwork.
	Return grilles sized 2X the area of the supply grills.
	Insulated ducts on outside (ie: ductwrap or ductboard) rather than interior lining.
	Check and calibrate sensors on air handling units annually (or more often if mfg specs recommend).
	Recommission air handler controls every 5 years.
	Check all control valves to ensure full closure and no leakage.
	Use only 2-way valves for all temperature control valves.
	Used fixed size pulleys for air handlers.
	Use direct drive fans (rather than belt driven).
	Use synchronous or cogged v belts to reduce slippage.

HVAC (Office) Best Practices

	Use air side economizers where appropriate climate conditions exist.
	Upgrade all existing VAV fan systems to utilize variable speed drives.
	Upgrade all office systems to Variable Air Volume with Variable Speed Drives.
	Use static pressure reset on any variable speed air handler supplying VAV terminal units.
	Vary AHU discharge (cooling) temperatures based on season to eliminate the need for reheat.
	Use CO_2 sensors to control outside air make up.
	Meet ASHRAE 62.1-2004 for indoor air quality (ventilation rate standards).
	Use MERV 13 filters or better in HVAC
	Design air diffuser air velocities for less than a NC (Noise Criteria) of 35.

Figure 35. Best practices checklist

The final piece was funding. Up to this point, any ideas to improve energy efficiency had to compete for funding with manufacturing expansion, reliability projects, or end-of-life replacement capital. We established a dedicated utility capital fund where resource (energy, water, other) efficiency projects could compete against each other. In theory, after some initial seed money this would fund itself from the savings of the previous projects. The first year we had $10M to allocate. There was such pent-up demand for the money that it was committed in well under a year. And the average payback of the projects was about 1.5 years—a 67% annual return on investment (ROI). The list of projects was kept in a spreadsheet/database and shared with all the sites. For key projects we would ask the sites to first assess if the project was applicable to their site and, if so, have them add it to their plans.

Metrics

As I mentioned, we also established metrics so we could establish the baseline and track our improvements. It took some time to make sure we had the right metrics. We wanted to make sure we measured energy and water use per unit of production. The hardest part of the metrics was trying to continually train management and bean counters to not spend much effort comparing one site to another. If you aren't familiar with the term bean counter, it's a person who works in finance. There are good bean counters and bad bean counters, just like managers or any other group. Bad ones only look at quarterly numbers and don't see the whole picture. They don't seem to realize the fastest way to improve quarterly numbers for the following years is to invest in efficiency this quarter. You would think a group that studied compound interest in college would grasp compound utility savings, but surprisingly some don't seem to get it. Sometimes they are under the wrath of a management directive to meet a certain number for the quarter, even if it drives them to intentionally make poor long-term decisions. It's just one of the systemic issues that prevents us from being as good as we can be.

The sites were different ages, sites, locations, climates, products, energy rates, and cultures. If you start comparing them to each other, then everyone will spend all their time making excuses and pointing out the reasons why their site is different. And most of those are valid reasons and aren't subject to change. We're not going to pick up a physical facility and move it to a better climate to improve the energy metrics. We kept stressing sites should be compared to themselves. Are they getting better versus where they were a year ago and making continuous improvement? That's what is important. Each site is competing against themselves to get better each year. Not to say there isn't some value in site to site comparisons. You can review site to site comparisons just to help know what the best possible performance is. We just tried to keep that as one point of data, but not let it become the focus of management. Even the best site should be able to keep getting better.

Developing valid metrics is a bit challenging. We needed energy and water per unit of production. You can also normalize to weather. Weather normalization might help some with site to site, but for large industrial facilities competing against their own data, the annual weather variations are often muted by the large internal load anyway. You have to look at your site and processes to understand if weather normalization has value.

In addition to the overall metrics, the sub-system metrics discussed in the "Best Practices" section are very valuable. These should be managed the same way—sites should strive to improve those metrics year over year. You can compare site to site to determine if there are some good practices that need to be shared.

And here's a twist—improvement is not always dependent on funding. Often, systems are operated in an inefficient manner. I've seen sites with no electronic monitoring use daily readings from manual gauges logged to a clipboard. They establish their baseline and make some system improvements and monitor for results. Which brings me back to the topic of measurement. No one likes to pay for quality measurement and monitoring systems, but everyone can benefit from a good system. Invest in high quality, high accuracy devices. If you are controlling your system to bad data, then you are intentionally operating it inefficiently. Good instrumentation, calibrated per the manufacturer recommendations, will give you the accurate data that allows you to fine-tune any system for better performance. I would rather have good data being recorded to a clipboard and typed into a spreadsheet than bad data feeding an automated control system that's forcing the system to operate inefficiently—even when it thinks it is doing the right thing.

Just as integrative design can be used to improve the operational efficiency of a new facility, an integrated approach to system operations can yield big benefits. Building and system engineers have certain valuable knowledge. Building operators have valuable knowledge. Maintenance mechanics have valuable knowledge. The best operational points are found when these functions team up to share ideas and develop system improvements. Installing an overly complex system no one knows how to maintain or operate is not the recipe for success.

A Few Examples

During my visits to various facilities around the world I found many "interesting" design and installation issues. There was an array of air handling units that had the control valve bypasses all open. When I asked about it, I was told over the years the control valves failed and management didn't want to pay to replace them, so they just used the valve on the bypass to manually adjust the flow to try and control temperature. This led to a very poor delta T on the chilled water supplied by the chiller. This led to low efficiency of the chiller with very high pumping costs. It also put them in danger of drifting out of spec in the manufacturing space.

Then was the array of flex duct connecting to the HEPA filters. Using a very short section of flex duct for the final few feet is fine, but some of these were run for twenty or thirty feet. And they were bent, kinked, and squeezed through and around other ducts and equipment to the point that were almost completely pinched off. This caused high pressure drop—first from the inherent poor pressure drop of flex duct, and second from pinching and squeezing the duct down to narrow passages. This resulted in much higher fan energy use for each unit of air delivered.

There was another cost-saving measure I discovered, which did the exact opposite of saving cost. There was a fan system with two fans in parallel—one was a main and the other was a backup. Perhaps at one point they were operated together, but the current exhaust requirements only required one fan run. The site received funding to install variable speed drives (VSD) to run the fans together in parallel at a much lower speed. Because of the Cube Law, this would provide a significant energy savings and allow one fan to act as a quick backup if the other failed. Unfortunately, they tried to save money by placing both fans on a single VSD. The problem was that the fans had very different inlet and outlet conditions. One was fairly smooth with a low pressure drop, while the other had an undersized duct that had several sharp bends as it wrapped around a column. When both ran at the same speed, the one with the smooth conditions was doing all the work while the other was using energy to spin, but not contributing much, if any, appreciable flow. The correct solution was a VSD for each fan and a pressure sensor in the duct of each fan. This would allow the fans to each run at an optimum speed (which might be a different speed for each fan) to produce the same pressure and flow so both would contribute to optimizing the entire flow.

Results

The consistent application of these processes combined with continuous improvement led to some dramatic results. One of our metrics was total energy use per chip manufactured. In nine years we cut that number in half. Yes, we doubled our energy efficiency in nine years. The water metric of total water extracted per chip was cut in half in eleven years. We use the term extracted to denote water removed from the environment—usually purchased from a municipal water supply, but sometimes taken from a well. Water savings came from increased water reuse along with source use reduction efforts.

This corporate wide improvement was due to a combination of many of the things discussed above. First, we were building a few new factories that were significantly more efficient than the others. As they came on line and ramped up production they contributed to the improvements. Then, the slow and steady work to improve all of the existing factories began to pay dividends. Some of the existing factories even made some upgrades to manufacturing equipment, such as vacuum pumps, to contribute to the improvement.

Figure 36 shows the changes all relative to a 2005 baseline where everything is set to one. You can see that production more than doubled (increasing 165%). Note the energy use remained almost flat (up just 1% by 2017). That drove the energy per chip manufactured to 0.38 (or only 38% as much energy needed to make a chip as it did in 2005). Water and greenhouse gas emissions also made great progress.

To be honest, some of the improvement would have occurred had we done nothing for efficiency. As the product engineers figured out a way to make each chip smaller, we could fit more chips on a wafer. It took the same energy to process the wafer, but we yielded more chips, so the energy/chip number improved. We call it "chip shrink," and it probably accounts for about a third of the overall improvement. It doesn't improve the back-end assembly and test process, because they still must test and package every chip. Another third of the improvement came from the new factories we opened. They were much more efficient, and as their share of the overall production grew it helped improve the overall company efficiency. The final third came from the intentional project actions we took at all our existing facilities around the world. Those projects and process improvements made a big difference and were very cost effective.

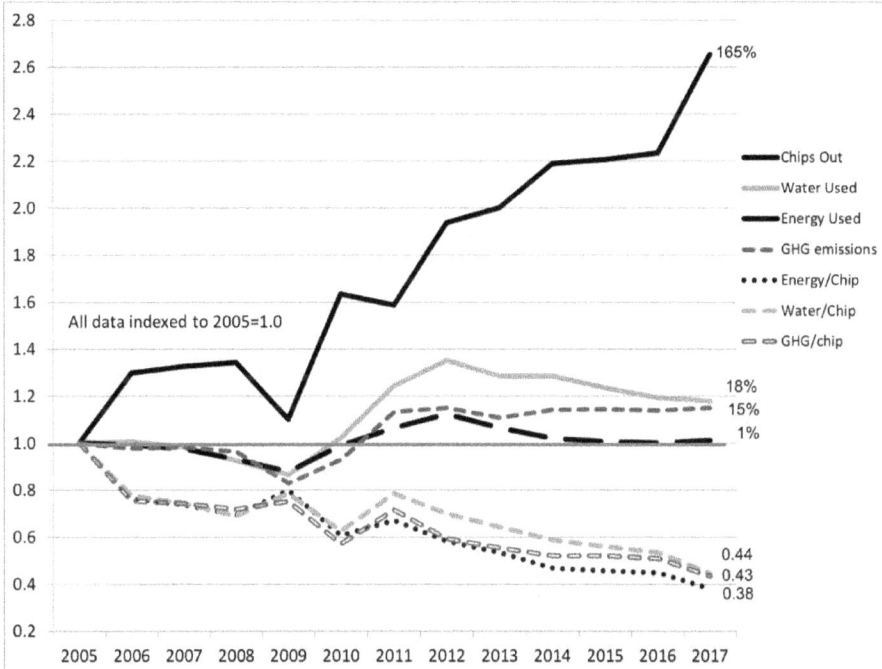

Figure 36. Production output compared to energy and water consumption and greenhouse gas emissions

When the utility bills are a couple of hundred million dollars per year and you can double your production with no increase in energy, you are saving a couple hundred million per year versus the business as usual scenario.

Large-Scale Renewable Energy

After all the of publicity that RFAB received, I became well known within our company. I received at least one email or phone call each week from an employee with an energy related question. Many of them were questions about their own house energy use. Some would ask why we didn't put large solar arrays on our building roofs, or large wind turbines in the parking lot. The simple and accurate answer was economics. We were still easily identifying numerous efficiency projects with payback of less than three years. Most solar and wind projects paid back in closer to ten years. I would always point out we needed to first reduce our use through efficiency, which is exactly what I did on my own house. When we ran out of good efficiency projects, we would then need a smaller renewable energy source to cover our requirements.

Not long before I retired an economical renewable energy option presented itself. A developer was planning a large wind farm in west Texas and offered our company the chance to purchase all the renewable energy output for twenty years at an extremely low price. It was a fixed price for twenty years that was much lower than the current price of our current grid mix of electricity. This wind farm would have covered a decent percentage of our Texas energy needs and lowered our global carbon footprint at a cost savings.

However, an executive who didn't "believe in climate change" turned the deal down. I'm still baffled that ideology apparently led to a decision that cost the company more money over the next twenty years. It was a final key factor that led me to retire.

The good news is many corporations are embracing the idea and shifting to renewable energy. RMI established a Business Renewables Center that has been helping make the connection between companies and renewable energy projects. Other companies are finding the cost of solar has fallen enough to install large on-site arrays at their facilities.

Corporate Change and Moving On

I worked at that company for over 33 years, most of them very good. For over a decade, I got to work on energy and resource efficiency at our sites around the world—and we made great progress and saved the company well over $50 million per year in utility costs. We achieved this with a lean management structure that trusted and empowered employees to take calculated risks and implement big improvements. These leaders listened to, and supported people in the organization. When some of those leaders retired, they were replaced by less visionary managers and a thick hierarchy.

There is an enormous difference between a manager and a leader. Leaders listen down the organization and seek to understand. Managers usually just listen up and try to do what pleases their boss. When this shift in management philosophy occurred and the upward-looking managers were put in place, input from the front lines of the organization was no longer rewarded. Instead, looking up the management chain and obediently following directions was rewarded. And most people do what is rewarded. Under this structure, it became unacceptable to challenge the executives—or even to inform them. The culture of the company seemed to change toward a culture of NO. Instead of exploring the possibilities of an idea, the answer just became NO. And there were layers of NO to get through. Some people seemed to lose any ability to critically analyze any idea—they just reacted with NO because they must have feared rocking the boat would hurt them in the rankings.

I could sense this backward slide in our corporate culture and was setting myself up for an early retirement. I had my finances in order to allow me to do that. The final straw was when I was scolded for a scientific presentation on climate change as part of an internal Earth Day presentation. This presentation was given to a small internal team who oversaw our corporate citizenship report. I was told after that meeting that our CFO "didn't believe in climate change and I shouldn't talk about it." I was lowered in the rankings (yes, they still used that outdated top-ten, bottom-ten ranking system), which made me ineligible to renew my title of senior member of the technical staff. I was meeting or exceeding my performance goals in almost every area and helping save the company millions of dollars every year, but that didn't matter. A political issue overrode my performance.

I had my fill of being micromanaged in an organization moving backward. Shortly after I reached age 55 I took an early retirement. We had made great strides in energy and resource efficiency, but instead of continuing to make progress, we were remaining stagnant and there was nothing more I could do. It was an excellent decision and very liberating. It brought me great joy to be free of ignorance toward science and innovation. And that freedom was the result of decades of good, disciplined money management.

After retiring from the corporate world, I established my consulting company and have helped a few other companies unlock the power of efficiency. I chose the name RE:source. The RE stands for many different things: **R**adical **E**fficiency, **R**educe **E**nergy use; **R**esource Efficiency; **RE**duce, **RE**use, **RE**cycle; **R**enewable **E**nergy; **RE**volution; **RE**imagine; **RE**silience; **RE**liable; **RE**think; **RE**sidential **RE**design. My LLC is Radical Efficiency. https://resourcedesign.org

Conclusion

Efficiency has indeed been my superpower. It's allowed me to live a fun life, contribute positively to society, retire early, and so much more. You can do it too. Develop some marketing immunity. Be a doivist. Take a few steps, have some success, and build on that. Then plant some seeds for others. It's not that difficult. You just need to break a few old, bad habits and replace them with new, good habits.

Efficiency can improve your personal life in areas such as finances and health. You'll live better with less. Efficiency can improve your home so it's better for your health, your finances, and the planet. Efficiency at work can make for a better and more profitable place to work while reducing your company's impact on the environment.

Our society is using fossil fuel energy very inefficiently and in an unsustainable manner. The result is a rapidly altering climate of the earth that sustains us. I've presented a number of practical and profitable solutions that can be implemented right away. Our family has made a tremendous reduction in our energy and resource use and we're better off financially because of those actions. I helped a large corporation improve their energy and resource efficiency and reduce their carbon footprint and it was very profitable.

Utilize as many of these solutions as you can to improve your personal and work life. Plan ahead, get ahead. The savings will start compounding quickly. If just a few people make improvements it doesn't change our current societal trajectory. If thousands, then millions, begin to act we'll start the transition toward a more sustainable and prosperous future for all of us.

About the Author: What Drives Me

When you see a person who is passionate about something, there's often a backstory of where that passion originated. Sometimes it's a single event, but often it's a combination of things. For most of my life I've taken the path less travelled. When everyone is going right, I'll often go left—but it's a conscientious choice, not a random wandering. I'm not just ambling down a trail or going a different way just to be different. My actions are the result of planning and thoughtfulness. It's a choice toward data and rational thinking instead of an emotional decision. And after several decades of doing this I have a good track record of success.

We all have a unique background. I was born to a single mother who was barely 18 years old. She dropped out of high school to have me. My dad got caught up with drugs, specifically heroin, so he was never in my life. One thing I got from my dad was an unpronounceable last name – Penouilh. I changed it to my mom's maiden name of Westbrook when I got married and it was an efficient decision. I save a lot of time now not having to tell people how to pronounce or spell my name. Mom and I lived with my maternal grandmother and grandfather when I was young. I was the first grandchild—and my grandfather had three girls, so I was not only his first grandchild, but the first boy in a generation. Word has it he spoiled me with daily trips to the toy store. He passed away when I was five—about the time my mom had my sister from a different dad. My sister's dad was not around for long, as he was a musician and always on the road. He and my mom divorced since they hardly saw each other. I barely remember him. Mom apparently decided she had had it with men and focused the rest of her days on creating a good home for my sister and me. I grew up around my mom, sister, grandmother, my mom's two sisters, and my four cousins—three of whom were girls. Is it any surprise I feel much more comfortable around women? I really didn't have a father figure in my life after my grandfather died when I was just five years old.

My mom ended up going to night school to finish high school (I was at her graduation) and then college for her bachelor's and master's degrees (again, I attended her graduation, and even a few classes with her as a child). She was a school teacher, elementary at first, then special education. She bought our first house when I was seven. The house was a new house in a new subdivision in south Louisiana—unincorporated Gretna, to be exact. The street was full of young families, many of them with four or five kids. There was always someone to play with, and we played outside all the time. Sports in the yard or street, riding bicycles to the woods or canal, and playing jailbreak until our parents made us come in at night. It was like growing up in a very large family.

Schools in Louisiana were not that great, so Mom always sacrificed to send us to private school. I begged to go to public school with my friends, and in seventh grade she let me—and it was not a good experience. With a November birthday, I was usually one of the youngest in the class, and I was small for my age. And I was a good student and in the band, which made me a prime target for bullies. It was a rough year. I went back to a small private school in eighth grade where bullies were less of a problem, and graduated from that school. I didn't rejoin the band when I started at the new school in 8th grade. My mom, who told me she always wished she had played in the band, found a clever way to get me to stick with band. In the first week of school the principal showed up at my classroom door and called me into the hallway. He and the band director were out there and asked me if I would be interested in joining the band. I was petrified, so I agreed. Thanks to mom for her creative approach that kept me playing saxophone.

Please don't equate my attendance at a private school with support for that type of system at the expense of our public schools. I fully support the public-school system. We need to focus our resources on establishing and protecting an efficient and well-run school system that serves everyone. An efficiently run system leaves more money for the teachers so we can attract the best candidates to serve those most in need of educational support.

Mom was a very pragmatic person and didn't seem to want for much. We had a nice home, car, and all the basics, but we didn't really have anything extravagant. Mom was a saver, not a spender. We always had a home-cooked meal and only ate out a couple of times per year. Mom liked to travel, and I was able to visit and see much of the country during the summers thanks to her summers off from teaching. It really instilled my love of nature to get to visit so many state and national parks. We vacationed in nature far more often than cities. She didn't make a lot of money, but she made sure that my sister and I would get a quality education and good exposure to the wider world.

I struggled deciding on what I wanted to major in at college. I was good at band and enjoyed it, and considered majoring in music and being a band director. I was a good student and liked science. My science fair projects were often related to the growing field of solar energy. I had a subscription to *Popular Science*, and I enjoyed learning about science and technology.

My mom gave me some advice one day that set the trajectory for my life. She told me teachers (and band directors) weren't paid very well and I was good at science, so I should consider science or engineering. She said if I didn't like it I could switch over to music. I liked solar thermal energy, and mechanical engineering seemed to be the best field for that.

Music played a bit of a role in my selection of a college. When I was in tenth grade we got a new band director who wanted to form a jazz ensemble, or stage band as they were called then. That director, Dennis Frantz, introduced me to some great music and taught me to improvise by ear. Then, our senior year of high school we got a new band director who had just graduated from Louisiana State University (LSU). Several of us were considering attending LSU. I was because they had programs for almost everything, which would allow me to start in engineering and switch if needed. Our band director, Tony Hicklen, asked us if we were planning to join the LSU Tiger Band. We were at a very small high school in south Louisiana, and it didn't occur to us we could be in a major college band. He assured us we would make it, and even set up the auditions for us. Thanks to his guidance, I majored in engineering but was able to play in both the marching band and basketball band. And I have continued to play saxophone in my role as president of a big band in Dallas, The Texas Instruments Jazz Band. (https://enerjazz.com/jazz). Music has remained an important part of my life. The creative side of jazz is an excellent brain balance for my science and engineering side.

The engineering path worked out, and I graduated college in December of 1982, shortly after President Reagan began dismantling the incentives and activity around renewable energy. President Carter had jump-started renewable energy after the oil crisis in the 1970s. However, there was no solar industry left by the time I graduated. The US unemployment rate the month I graduated was 10.8%. Despite good grades, I only had one job offer from a chemical refinery in Louisiana, and I wasn't too keen on taking that job. My mom encouraged me to go to graduate school until the job market picked up. Just before school started I got a call from a semiconductor company I had interviewed with in the fall. They said they had the approval to do some hiring and wondered if I was still available. They flew me to Dallas and the interview went well, but it was going to be about a week before they could let me know anything. I attended graduate school for three days, then the call came with a job offer. And that's how I ended up in Dallas in January of 1983.

Efficiency is somewhat ingrained in me. I've disliked waste since I was a kid and have constantly looked for simpler and better ways to do things. I cleaned my plate at every meal. I was an old soul who could identify with an older generation's Depression-era sensibilities—though I was born in 1960. I also recognized connectedness from an early age. I've always been a whole systems thinker.

How we see ourselves is sometimes different from what others observe. A writer for *Dallas CEO* magazine described me like this: "He is, in short, an unassuming, likable, multitalented nerd." (https://www.resourcedesign.org/wp-content/uploads/2015/06/Article-from-Dallas-CEO-publication.pdf)